HOLDEMAN CHURCH PROPERTY

JUNIOR HYMNS

For Juniors in
Church, Sunday School, and
Summer Bible School

WALTER E. YODER, EDITOR

All glory, laud and honor
To Thee, Redeemer, King!
To whom the lips of children
Made sweet hosannas ring.

—THEODULPH.

HERALD PRESS

SCOTTDALE, PENNSYLVANIA

Foreword

The purpose of this small book of hymns arranged in three parts for children's voices is to make material available so we can teach our Juniors to sing well in parts, as well as to furnish good hymns for the worship services. We know it is possible to teach juniors to sing in three parts, and this will give them much more beautiful singing in the department. It will also help to prepare them for participation in the singing of the congregation. There may be those who feel they cannot cultivate part singing. For those we would say, it will be worth some effort to try, and then if found impossible, we feel that you will still profit by using these hymns instead of many of the lighter choruses that are often used.

In our established churches we desire to cultivate an appppreciation of the great hymns of the Christian church. These hymns, having come out of the experiences of the Christians of the past, can become a source of strength for our young Christians of today. This, too, will do much to preserve and develop the best type of singing in our congregations. We send this forth with a hope and a prayer that through the use of these hymns among the juniors the church may be made to prosper in its service of song.

—WALTER E. YODER.

PRINTED
IN U·S·A

Singing With the Juniors

Part Singing

This little hymnbook is an attempt to answer the problem of what music to use with our juniors in summer Bible school as well as in Sunday school and in Sunday evening junior meetings. We have been satisfied too long with singing primary songs and easy sentimental choruses with our juniors. We need only to study the various courses of music used in the public schools, in grades four to eight, to be convinced that these growing children can sing beautifully in parts. Part singing with our juniors is a new undertaking in most of our churches. All observing song leaders have seen and heard both boys and girls sing alto, but have been slow to use this talent in a definite way to build junior hymn singing. We believe that the office of music belongs to the congregation. We believe congregational singing the most appropriate use of music in the church, because all may unite in this act of worship, and by the blending of all the voices we lift our hearts in worship and praise and prayer. Earlier our forefathers sang in unison. Many of their old songs were sung with fine interpretation and expression, but with the advancement of musical knowledge through the singing schools of the past and the public schools of the present we have been taught to sing in parts. We have a style and type of singing in the Mennonite Church that is peculiar to our own tradition and training. We sing in four parts and without accompaniment of instruments. From the standpoint of worship music, there is no purer style than this, and we hope that by training our boys and girls to sing in parts we can develop and preserve this pure style of church music. We hope also that the interest in singing will be greatly enhanced by this new experience.

Dividing the Group for Three-part Singing

The children should be divided into three groups for the music study and singing. They should also keep this seating arrangement for the worship hour so that they will get more practice in singing together. The more mature lower voices of the girls, and the older boys whose voices are beginning to show signs of changing, or at least are low enough to sing the part, should be placed on the lowest part. There need not be many; possibly ten per cent of the entire group will be enough. It will not take them very long to feel the lowest part if they have one or two good readers in the group or if they have some older person to help them learn the part. It will be well at first to have one of the teachers sing with this group, either a low alto or a high tenor. There are usually quite a number of sixth to eighth

3

grade girls who like to sing alto. Select from this group, those who have the best ears and who can read music quite well to sing the middle part. The middle voice is the most difficult part to learn; therefore use your best musicians on this part. Again the group need not be large, possibly twenty per cent of the entire group. If you have fifty boys and girls in this department, you should have from five to ten on the lowest part, ten to fifteen on the middle part, and all the others singing soprano. Certainly, the largest number should be singing soprano, and with a number of good voices on the two lower parts, we add harmony to melody and we train our children to sing in parts. Make the children's singing sound like chorus singing, and thay will take a great interest in the new undertaking.

Teaching Three-part Songs

To begin in this new experience use some old hymns like "Above the Trembling Elements," "Somebody Did a Golden Deed," and "My Jesus, I Love Thee." If possible, have a teacher who sings well to sit in each part to help keep it going and to help the children with true pitches, for some children may simply sing by ear and not stay on one part accurately. Teachers doing this must be careful to sing with a light tone, and not too loudly. Use the kind of tone the children should use.

Teaching a New Song

1. Motivate the song by telling the children something about the song and its message, or its author or composer. Read the hymn and note the beauty and meaning of the words. If there are phrases or words that need explaining, take time to do so.

2. Notice the time signature, and then read the words in unison in time of the music. This will clear up all difficult rhythm patterns.

3. Notice the key signature; then give the exact pitch to all the parts and have them hum the first chord. Then, using a neutral syllable like "la," sing through the song with an easy tempo, letting the children follow the notes carefully. With a teacher on each part, you will be surprised how soon the children will learn a new song.

4. If the song is too difficult to teach all three parts at once, take up each part alone with the children of each section. That is, the teacher will sing the soprano for the children while the children listen; then invite them to join with the teacher, singing quietly until they can carry their part alone. Then use the same method on the two alto parts; sing each part alone for the children and then ask them to sing along quietly with you. Experience in public-school work has taught us that this is effective. After all of the parts have been treated thus try putting the parts together, singing through first with "la," and then singing the song with the words.

The Child Voice

Since beautiful singing holds an important place in our worship, it is time we are doing much more to train our boys and girls to sing well—that is, to sing with a beautiful tone, in exact time and pitch, and with expression. The natural, free, unforced tone of the child is most beautiful. The tone of the unchanged voice is light, sweet, and high. Some song leaders who have not studied the child voice make a great mistake when they urge the children to sing loudly. When the child tries to sing loudly, he uses a coarse, chesty, forced tone which is not beautiful, neither is it the true singing voice of the child. Encourage him, rather, to sing sweetly and with expression. Do not allow the small child to sing with a shouting tone. The tones of the older girls singing alto may be a little heavier, and more resonant. The tones of the older boys may be a little rough, which is a sign that the voice is beginning to change. Some boys try to sing bass before the voice changes. This is a great mistake. Encourage them to sing soprano, for otherwise they will only develop a sort of monotone. And what shall we do with the monotone? We must try, first of all, to train him to use his singing voice. The singing voice is higher than the speaking voice; therefore teach him to use his high tones. See if he can imitate a siren, using "oo" as in moon. Sing it very high and light. All young boys should learn to sing soprano. There should be no monotones in the junior department if the beginner and primary departments have done their work well in teaching children to sing. Do not have monotone teachers in the beginner or primary departments, because we need teachers there who can help the little children to sing. This, certainly, is a very important part of the training of the small child. There may remain a few monotones after we have done all we can to teach them to sing. If these remain in the singing group, be sure that they sing very quietly so that they do not disturb the good singers and also that they do not destroy the beauty of the music. Let the nonsinger do something else in the worship period besides sing. Let him read the scripture, a prayer, a poem, or a story. Then ask him not to sing out loud with the group since his voice does not blend with the others. He will not feel hurt if he is given an important part outside of the singing exercise. Let every song leader remember that when he is working with children of grades four to eight he has the child voice at its best, a voice most beautiful and simple, yet most expressive when singing sacred music.

Exercises for Training the Child Voice

1. One of the best exercises we can use with children is to sing familiar songs which have been memorized, using the neutral syllable "ah" as in far, or "oh" as in row, or "oo" as in moon. Sing in unison, being sure everyone sings with freedom, using a smooth light tone. Then sing with the three parts, this time watching for pure harmony. Be sure everyone is alert and giving attention to the blending of voices.

2. Sing scales and chord figures: do, ti, la, sol, fa, me, re, do; do, sol, mi, do; do, mi, sol, do; do, la, fa, re; do, mi, sol; do, la, fa; sol, ti, re, do. If a blackboard is available, put these figures on the board and sing from the board. Drill in different keys.

3. In order to develop good clear pronunciation of the words, sing the words of a familiar song on one pitch in the time of the music. Be sure they use a very smooth tone and the same good singing quality they use when singing vowels. This is a good thing to do when you want them to sing their words more clearly.

4. Teach them to sing all their songs using the sol-fa syllables. Even the old familiar songs should be sung with the syllables, because it teaches the tonal relationship between the tones of the scale.

5. Sing two- and three-part rounds, with words first, then with neutral syllables.

6. Vocalize the chords of any of your songs. The following are the chords from "O worship the Lord." Any chorister can pick out the chords of any simple hymn for use in this way. Sing very slowly.

Vocalize the song, "Hear Our Prayer, O Lord," using various neutral syllables.

Position in Singing

It is essential that hymn singers be alive physically, alert mentally, and quickened spiritually. Everything that will assist in bringing about this condition is worthy and must be considered.

Ventilation and lighting must be adequate. Fresh air always makes singing easier, and helps the singers to stay on pitch. Fresh air tones up the physical body, and thus improves the spirit and enhances the health of the group. Temperature is also important. The room should not be too warm, because singers always warm up with the exercise of singing. A temperature of about sixty-seven is warm enough for the singers but may be a little cool for the congregation. Lighting is equally important. Insufficient light is depressing, and too bright or glaring light is tiresome. We should try to get the right amount of light to shine on the copies for the singers and also show the leader's face and hands. This will establish a proper relationship and mood between leader and singers for good rehearsals or programs.

Sitting in an erect position with chest at a good medium height is best for good singing. Children should hold books high enough to be able to see the song leader and the song at the same time. The singers must be taught to throw their voices out and up, not down into their books or into the seat in front of them. Singing with chins up and faces aglow with the joyous spirit of song will help to make the music and worship hour one of pleasure and profit to both leader and pupil. If the standing position is preferred, see that the children stand erect, not slouched down or standing on one leg, as some do. Stand as if ready to go on a march. Remember, singers must be alive and must not be allowed to take a passive attitude or to be in a restful mood. Sitting and standing in an erect position produces and encourages proper breathing habits, which are essential to good singing.

A joyous mental attitude is also essential for good singing. A grouchy, sour song leader will get nothing accomplished with a music group. Rehearsals are to be enjoyed. The right kind of singing leads to happiness, and happiness leads to good singing. Make the music hour in the summer Bible school a joyous hour.

Being quickened spiritually by the power of the crucified and risen Lord is the experience that brings joy to the human heart. The inspiration of this knowledge is the source of all Christian song. It is this joy that must be reflected in the hymns we sing. Lead the children to see this truth. Help them to see that the truth of the Word is expressed in the great hymns of he church, and for that reason they should memorize many of them.

Pronunciation

Pronunciation is one of the important elements in beautiful singing. We do not care to listen to singers who do not say their words clearly and distinctly. To sing with an accurate pronunciation of the words, requires alert ears to hear the sounds in detail, and a wide-awake mind that is desirous of making improvements and developing a good singing voice.

Pronunciation depends first of all upon the singing of pure vowel sounds. Tone is sustained in the vowel. The quality of the tone and the purity of the tone are both determined by the way the vowels are sung. Resonance and a feeling of purity in the timbre of the tone depend on correct singing of the vowel sound. There are four primary vowel sounds, and all other vowel sounds in the English language come from these four basic vowels. Taking them up in the order of greatest resonance and brilliance, the "e" comes first. We find this sound in words like "sleep," "seen." This vowel is sounded well to the front of the mouth. When sung, the upper teeth should show in a pleasant facial expression. The tone produced is very brilliant, and if properly sung, the "e" will give a spinning tone of great beauty and carrying power.

The second vowel is the "a" as found in words like "may," "day." It has more fullness than the "e" and is a little broader and deeper. Many people have difficulty singing the "a" in its pure sound. That is, they sing a sound that seems to be a cross between the pure "a" and the "e." Teachers must watch carefully that the children sing these two vowels with purity of quality. Watch carefully that these two vowels remain brilliant and do not take on a muffled quality.

The third vowel is the "a" as found in the word "father." This vowel produces a joyous tone, and gives the face a pleasant expression. The mouth must be wide open with the feeling of a little smile, the throat also wide open, and the tongue somewhat concave. Here we have a tone that opens the mouth and throat more than any other vowel, and with such an open, relaxed position the tone can roll out in great power and beauty.

The fourth of these primary vowels is the "o" as in "row." This vowel has a tendency to be dark in color. A good impression of this vowel when singing it, is that you are singing through a cylinder which is placed against the roof of the mouth. Endeavor to keep this vowel as brilliant as possible, not allowing it to fall back into the throat but feeling it forward on the hard palate. It is a rich, round tone which this vowel produces. A good exercise to even up these vowels and keep the "o" brilliant is the following:

me _ _ _ _ _ _ āy _ _ _ _ _ _ _ äh _ _ _ _ _ _ _ _ ōh _ _ _ _ _ _ _ _

There are some variations of these primary vowel sounds which are just as important as the primaries. Possibly the most abused and misused of these is the short "i" as found in such words as "is," "with." The tendency in most church singing is for this sound to be an impure, very dull, colorless tone, having no character or resonance. The correct sound for the short "i" comes from the primary "e." Hold the mouth as for the pure "e," keeping the tone focused to the front of the mouth. Retain that spinning quality which was so prominent in the "e." Now sound the short "i"; then prolong that sound and you should have it. Next practice singing words containing the short "i," "is," "in."

Another vowel that needs some consideration is the short "a" as in "land" or "thanks." Maintain the position as for "ah" as in "father" but think short "a" as you would in speech. Do not say "lawnd" which is a tendency in some voices. Another tendency is to sound the "n" too soon. The "a" must be sung to the end of the note, leaving just enough time to add the "nd" quickly at the very end.

The "oo" as in "soon" or "moon" is a good vowel to use with children's voices. The primary "o" is the basis for this sound. Keep the mouth well rounded and the tone well forward so that the tone produced will have life and character. This is a good sound to use in the place of humming when you are using a solo with chorus accompaniment; have the chorus sing "oo."

Not only do we need pure vowels in beautiful singing, but we also need clear-cut consonant sounds. The letters at the beginning and ending of words need to be given just enough stress to make the words clear and distinct. Some of the consonants have pitch, such as "m," "n," "l," "y," "d." Great care must be taken that the group of singers do not change pitch on these final consonants. Be sure also that the proper sound be given to the consonants—that "Lord" does not sound like "Lort," and "Kings" like "Kinks." Usually children have very little difficulty with pronunciation of words, but let us as song leaders be careful to maintain and develop clear enunciation of words so that our juniors will attain good singing habits.

Interpretation of Hymns

Hymn singing becomes a joyous experience for both old and young when the music is well sung and music and words have been given proper interpretation. Several important points must now be considered in regard to interpretation. Of first importance is the tempo, or speed, with which the song is sung. Some song leaders sing all songs and hymns with a fast tempo. They want to put pep into the music. Other people think music is used as a call to march into the services. Now these ideas are all wrong. The purpose of music is a means of worship. We do not need marching or pep as an element in our worship. We need, in our worship, a quiet contemplation of God and His power, love, and mercy. Let us endeavor to make our hymn singing fit into such a program and spirit. Fast singing of hymns is paralyzing to an audience and gives no thought to the interpretation of the words or music. Singing too slowly is also bad. Every hymn has a tempo that is best, and a good chorister will study each hymn with a purpose to determine the speed for the song. In connection with the tempo there is also the time element. Keep the rhythm rolling along evenly so that your group will have no difficulty in singing together. Also watch the rhythm patterns and bring them out clearly, and where there is imitation be sure to make these clear-cut. Some common markings for tempo follow:

Allegro	meaning	moderately fast
Vivace	meaning	lively
Presto	meaning	very fast
Moderato	meaning	with moderate speed
Adagio	meaning	slow
Lento	meaning	slow
Largo	meaning	slow and with stately motion
Andante	meaning	moderately slow and in singing style

Ritard	musical sign—rit.	meaning	gradually slower
Rallentando	musical sign—rall.	meaning	gradually faster
Accelerando	musical sign—accel.	meaning	gradually faster
Stringendo	musical sign—string.	meaning	gradually slower

Another point in interpretation has to do with power in singing. **Children** should never be uged to sing loudly, but still there must be some **variety** in power. All art must have variety for the sake of beauty. The artist **never** selects a prairie as his model for an art picture, unless it be a **rolling** prairie. As a rule he desires mountains, with streams of water, clouds, **and** trees. In the same way, if our hymn singing is to be beautiful and **artistic,** there must be variety, not less in degree than a rolling prairie. Translated into musical terms this would mean the use of the "swell" as the basis **for** all interpretation. This does not mean that our music should sound like accordion music, because in that type of music there is no variety of pattern. There is, however, no time when the swell is entirely absent in artistic singing or playing. Every hymn phrase must be given its own variation of power so as to give proper emphasis to important words and enhance the spirit and meaning of the hymn. Every hymn should have its quieter places, as well as its principal climax. Song leaders should study the hymns in order to determine these points. Praise and thanksgiving hymns will be sung with greater power than evening hymns, or hymns of sorrow such as the passion hymns. But whether they be hymns of joy or hymns of sorrow, watch for the places where variety can be brought in and where important words can be given proper emphasis. There is no finer piece of art in the smaller compositions than a fine hymn wedded to an equally fine **tune** and sung by an inspired chorus or audience. It is a challenge to **every** chorister to lead and inspire his singers to sing the great hymns of **the** church with spirit and understanding. We have selected many of the **great** hymns of the church for this little book. We believe there is nothing **better** for the children to learn and to memorize than these hymns, together **with** the assigned scripture passages.

The editor has marked a number of hymns as suggestions for interpretation. There is no hard and set rule for this; in fact, with every new condition there may be a new and more expressive interpretation. These hymns have been marked in order to give to choristers some ideas, and it is hoped they will carefully work out their own interpretation. See the following:

Here are a few of the most common power markings and their meaning:

Forte	musical sign	f	meaning	loud
Fortissimo	musical sign	ff	meaning	very loud
Mezzo forte	musical sign	mf	meaning	medium loud
Mezzo	musical sign	m	meaning	medium power
Mezzo piano	musical sign	mp	meaning	medium soft
Piano	musical sign	p	meaning	soft
Pianissimo	musical sign	pp	meaning	very soft
Diminuendo	musical sign	dim.	meaning	gradually softer
Crescendo	musical sign	cresc.	meaning	gradually louder

O Come, Let Us Worship

Ps. 95:6

WALTER E. YODER

1

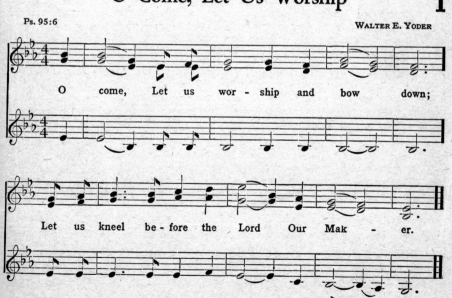

O come, Let us wor - ship and bow down;

Let us kneel be - fore the Lord Our Mak - er.

2 Enter Into His Gates

Psalms 100

WALTER E. YODER

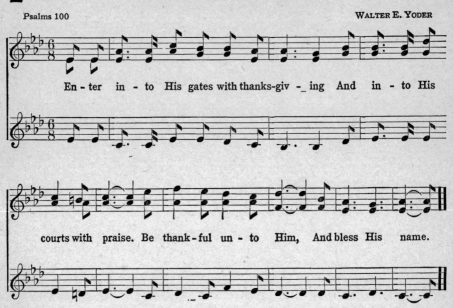

En - ter in - to His gates with thanks-giv - ing And in - to His

courts with praise. Be thank-ful un - to Him, And bless His name.

3 O Worship the Lord

Bible

WALTER E. YODER

O wor - ship the Lord, In the beau - ty of ho - li - ness

O give thanks un - to the Lord, For He is good.

God, That Madest Earth and Heaven

Ar Hyd Nos

REGINALD HEBER
FREDERICK HOSMER

Welsh Folk Tune
Arr. by W. E. YODER

1. God that mad - est earth and heav - en, Dark - ness and light;
2. When the con - stant sun re - turn - ing, Dark - ness and light;

Who the day for toil hast giv - en, For rest the night;
May we, born a - new like morn - ing, To la - bor rise;

May Thine an - gel - guards de - fend us, Slum - ber sweet Thy
Gird us for the task that calls us, Let not ease and

mer - cy send us; Ho - ly dreams and hopes at-tend us, This live - long night.
self en-thrall us, Strong thru Thee what-e'er be-fall us, O God most wise.

5   Hear Our Prayer O Lord

GEORGE WHELPTON

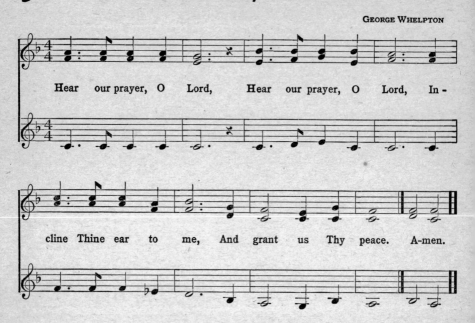

Hear our prayer, O Lord, Hear our prayer, O Lord, In-
cline Thine ear to me, And grant us Thy peace. A-men.

6   Let Us With a Gladsome Mind

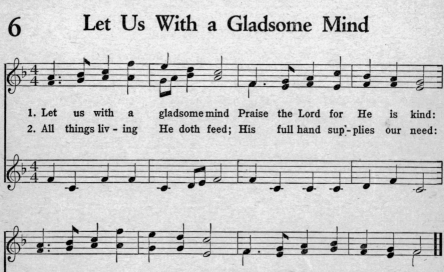

1. Let us with a gladsome mind Praise the Lord for He is kind:
2. All things liv-ing He doth feed; His full hand sup'-plies our need:

For His mer-cy shall en-dure, Ev-er faith-ful, ev-er sure.

My Jesus, I Love Thee

London Hymn book

7

A. J. GORDON

1. My Jesus, I love Thee, I know Thou art mine; For
2. I love Thee be - cause Thou hast first lov - ed me, And
3. I will love Thee in life, I will love Thee in death, And
4. In man - sions of glo - ry and end - less de - light, I'll

Thee all the fol - lies of sin I re - sign; My
pur - chased my par - don on Cal - va - ry's tree; I
praise Thee as long as Thou lend - est me breathe; And
ev - er a - dore Thee in heav - en so bright; I'll

gra - cious Re - deem - er, my Sav - iour art Thou, If
love Thee for wear - ing the thorns on Thy brow; If
say when the death - dew lies cold on my brow, If
sing with the glit - ter - ing crown on my brow, If

ev - er I loved Thee, my Je - sus, 'tis now.
ev - er I loved Thee, my Je - sus, 'tis now.
ev - er I loved Thee, my Je - sus, 'tis now.
ev - er I loved Thee, my Je - sus, 'tis now.

8 Thou Life Within My Life

ELIZA SCUDDER

JOHN B. DYKES
Arr. WALTER E. YODER

1. Thou life with-in my life, Than self more near,
2. Take part with me a-gainst These doubts that rise
3. How shall I call Thee who Art al-ways near?

Thou veil-ed pres-ence in-fin-ite-ly clear;
And seek to throne Thee far in dis-tant skies;
How shall I praise Thee who art still most dear?

From all my name-less wea-ri-ness I flee
Take part with me a-gainst this self that dares
What may I give Thee save what Thou hast given,

To find my cen-tre and my rest in Thee.
As-sume the bur-den of these sins and cares.
And whom but Thee have I in earth or Heaven?

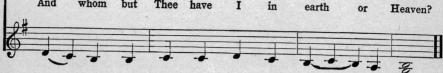

10 There Is a Name I Love

F. WHITFIELD

H. W. GREATOREX

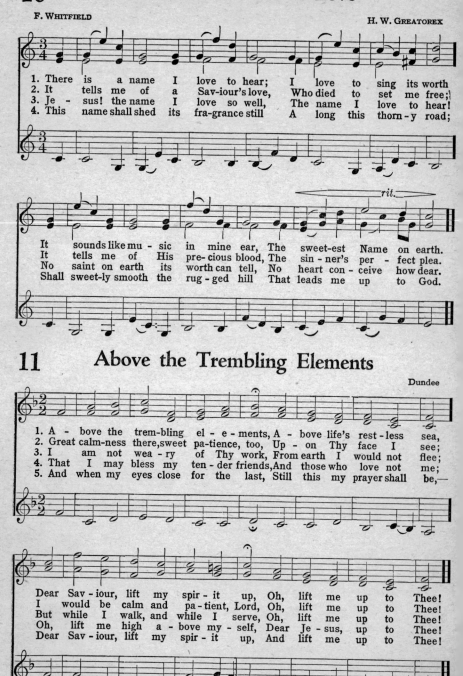

1. There is a name I love to hear; I love to sing its worth
2. It tells me of a Sav-iour's love, Who died to set me free;
3. Je - sus! the name I love so well, The name I love to hear!
4. This name shall shed its fra-grance still A long this thorn-y road;

It sounds like mu - sic in mine ear, The sweet-est Name on earth.
It tells me of His pre-cious blood, The sin - ner's per - fect plea.
No saint on earth its worth can tell, No heart con-ceive how dear.
Shall sweet-ly smooth the rug - ged hill That leads me up to God.

11 Above the Trembling Elements

Dundee

1. A - bove the trem-bling el - e-ments, A - bove life's rest-less sea,
2. Great calm-ness there, sweet pa-tience, too, Up - on Thy face I see;
3. I am not wea - ry of Thy work, From earth I would not flee;
4. That I may bless my ten - der friends, And those who love not me;
5. And when my eyes close for the last, Still this my prayer shall be,—

Dear Sav - iour, lift my spir - it up, Oh, lift me up to Thee!
I would be calm and pa - tient, Lord, Oh, lift me up to Thee!
But while I walk, and while I serve, Oh, lift me up to Thee!
Oh, lift me high a - bove my - self, Dear Je - sus, up to Thee!
Dear Sav - iour, lift my spir - it up, And lift me up to Thee!

In the Morning

CHARLES NEFF

Melody by CHARLES NEFF
Harmonized by W. E. YODER

In the morn - ing I will lift up mine eyes un - to my

Sav - iour, In the morn - ing I will lift up my

voice to sing His praise. In the morn - ing I will

of - fer my - self to do His bid - ding That

I may sing for Christ my king, the whole day through.

13 Thou Art My Shepherd

M. E. THALHEIMER

J. CRAMER

1. Thou art my Shep - herd Car - ing for all my need,
2. If Thou wilt guide me, Glad - ly I'll go with Thee;

Thy lit - tle lamb to feed, Trust - ing Thee still.
No harm can come to me, Hold - ing Thy hand.

In the green pas - tures low Where liv - ing wa - ters flow.
And soon my wea - ry feet Safe in the gold - en street,

Safe by Thy side I go, Fear - ing no ill.
Where all who love Thee meet, Re - deemed shall stand.

Unto the Hills

ALBERT L. PEACE
arr. WALTER E. YODER

1. Un - to the hills a - round do I lift up My long - ing
2. Je - ho - vah is Him - self thy keep - er true, From ev - 'ry
3. From ev - 'ry e - vil shall He keep thy soul, From ev - 'ry

eyes O whence for me shall my sal - va - tion come
sin; Je - ho - vah thy de - fense on thy right hand
sin; Je - ho - vah shall pre - serve thy go - ing out,

From whence a - rise? From God the Lord doth come my cer - tain
Him - self hath made. And Thee no sun by day shall ev - er
Thy com - ing in. A - bove thee watch - ing, He whom we a -

aid; From God, the Lord, Who heav'n and earth hath made.
smite No moon shall harm thee in the si - lent night.
dore Shall keep thee hence-forth, Yea, for - ev - er - more.

15 God Calls Me to the Hour of Prayer

HELEN BOARDMAN KNOX

WALTER E. YODER

1. God calls me to the hour of prayer, Far from the world a - part, Where
2. God calls me to the hour of prayer, Where deep with - in the breast, Far

I may hear His voice, that speaks To ev - 'ry lis - t'ning heart.
from the world's mad tu - - mult, I find sweet joy and rest.

REFRAIN

O, bless-ed bless-ed hour of prayer, Where life re-newed is found, Where

peace and love and power di - vine for ev-er more - - - - a-bound.

For ever more a-bound.

To Thee O Lord, I Lift Mine Eyes 16

"THE 541 HYMN"

Psalm 123

ROBERT LOWERY

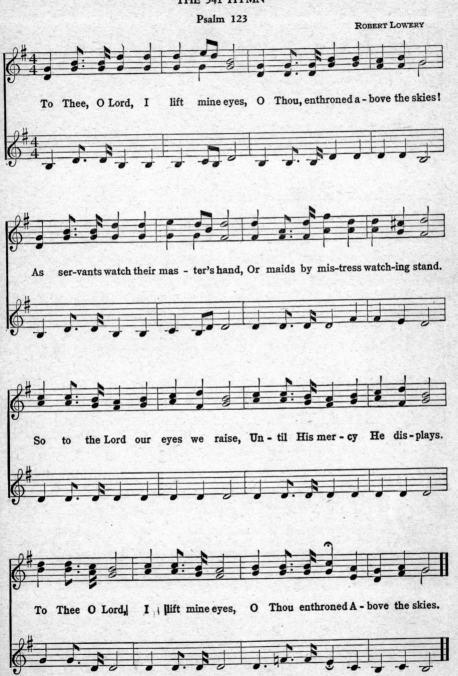

To Thee, O Lord, I lift mine eyes, O Thou, enthroned a-bove the skies!

As ser-vants watch their mas - ter's hand, Or maids by mis-tress watch-ing stand.

So to the Lord our eyes we raise, Un - til His mer - cy He dis-plays.

To Thee O Lord, I lift mine eyes, O Thou enthroned A - bove the skies.

17 Vesper Hymn

Samuel Longfellow

Dimitri S. Bortnyansky
Arr. W. E. Yoder

1. Now, on land and sea de-scend-ing Brings the night its peace pro-found;
2. Soon as dies the sun-set glo-ry, Stars of heav'n shine out a-bove;
3. As the dark-ness deep-ens o'er us, Lo, e-ter-nal stars a-rise;

Let our ves-per hymn be blend-ing With the ho-ly calm a-round.
Tell-ing still the an-cient sto-ry Their Cre-a-tor's changeless love
Hope and faith and love rise glo-rious, Shin-ing in the spir-it's skies.

Ju-bi-la-te! Ju-bi-la-te! Ju-bi-la-te, A-men.
Ju-bi-la-te, Ju-bi-la-te, Ju-bi-la-te, A-men.
Ju-bi-la-te, Ju-bi-la-te, Ju-bi-la-te, A-men.

Alto Solo

Let our ves-per hymns be blend-ing With a ho-ly calm a-round.
Tell-ing still the an-cient sto-ry Their Cre-a-tor's changeless love.
Hope and faith and love rise glo-rious, Shin-ing in the spir-it's skies.

Hum - - - - - Hum - - - - -

After last stanza repeat 3rd score. Jubilate Amen.

Come, Thou Almighty King

CHARLES WESLEY

FELICE DE GIARDINI

1. Come, Thou Al - might - y King, Help us Thy name to sing, Help us to praise: Fa - ther, all - glo - ri - ous, O'er all vic - to - ri - ous, Come, and reign o - ver us, An - cient of Days.

2. Come, Thou In - car - nate Word, Gird on Thy might - y sword, Our prayer at - tend: Come, and Thy peo - ple bless, And give Thy word suc - cess: Spir - it of ho - li - ness, On us de - scend.

3. Come, Ho - ly Com - fort - er, Thy sa - cred wit - ness bear In this glad hour: Thou who al - might - y art, Now rule in ev - 'ry heart, And ne'er from us de - part, Spir - it of pow'r.

4. To the great One in Three E - ter - nal prais - es be Hence ev - er - more: His sov - 'reign maj - es - ty May we in glo - ry see, And to e - ter - ni - ty Love and a - dore.

19 Now the Day Is Over

SABINE BARING-GOULD
JOSEPH BARNBY

1. Now the day is o - ver, Night is draw-ing nigh;
2. Je - sus, grant the wea - ry Calm and sweet re - pose;
3. Grant to lit - tle chil - dren Vi - sions bright of Thee;
4. Thro' the long night watch - es May Thine an - gels spread
5. When the morn - ing wak - ens, Then may I a - rise

dim. *pp*

Shad - ows of the eve - ning Steal a - cross the sky.
With Thy ten - d'rest bless - ing May our eye - lids close.
Guard the sail - ors toss - ing On the deep, blue sea.
Their white wings a - bove me, Watch - ing round my bed.
Pure, and fresh, and sin - less In Thy ho - ly eyes.

pp

20 Fairest Lord Jesus
CRUSADER'S HYMN

German 17th Century
Arr. by WALTER E. YODER

1. Fair-est Lord Je - sus! Rul - er of all na - ture! O Thou of God and man the Son!
2. Fair are the meadows, Fair - er still the woodlands, Robed in the blooming garb of spring;
3. Fair is the sunshine, Fair - er still the moonlight, And fair the twinkling star - ry hosts;

Thee will I cher - ish Thee will I hon - or, Thou my soul's glory, joy, and crown!
Je - sus is fair - er, Je - sus is pur - er, Who makes the woeful heart to sing.
Je - sus shines brighter, Je - sus shines pur - er, Than all the angels heaven can boast. Amen.

Jesus, Friend of Little Children

21

WALTER J. MATHAMS

J. H. MAUNDER

1. Je - sus, Friend of lit - tle chil - dren Be a friend to me;
2. Teach me how to grow in good - ness Dai - ly as I grow;

Take my hand and ev - er keep me Close to Thee.
Thou hast been a child, and sure - ly Thou dost know.

Jesus, Friend of Little Children

22

WALTER J. MATHAMS

1. Je - sus, friend of lit - tle chil - dren, Be a friend to me;
2. Teach me how to grow in good-ness Dai - ly as I grow;

Take my hand and ev - er keep me close to Thee.
Thou hast been a child, and sure - ly Thou dost know.

23 Hushed Was the Evening Hymn
(SAMUEL)

JAMES D. BURNS

ARTHUR S. SULLIVAN

1. Hushed was the eve-ning hymn, The tem-ple courts were dark, The lamp was burn-ing dim Be-fore the sa-cred ark; When sud-den-ly a Voice di-vine Rang through the si-lence of the shrine.

2. O give me Sam-uel's ear: The o-pen ear, O Lord, A-live and quick to hear Each whis-per of Thy word! Like him to an-swer at Thy call, And to o-bey Thee first of all.

1. Fa - ther we thank Thee for the night,
2. Help us to do the things we should,

And for the plea - sant morn - ing light.
To be to oth - ers kind and good;

For rest and food and lov - ing care.
In all our work, and all our play,

And all that makes the day so fair.
To love Thee bet - ter ev - ery day.

25 I Would Love Thee

MADAME GUYON

Hymns and Tunes

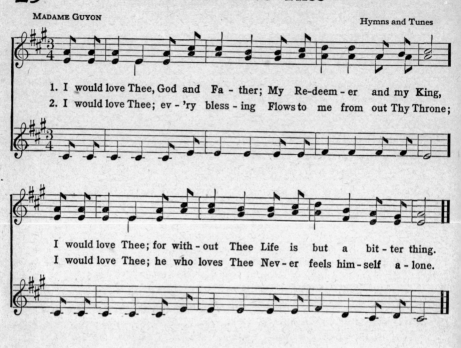

1. I would love Thee, God and Fa - ther; My Re-deem - er and my King,
2. I would love Thee; ev - 'ry bless - ing Flows to me from out Thy Throne;

I would love Thee; for with - out Thee Life is but a bit - ter thing.
I would love Thee; he who loves Thee Nev - er feels him - self a - lone.

26 Jesus Tender Shepherd Hear Me

MARY L. DUNCAN

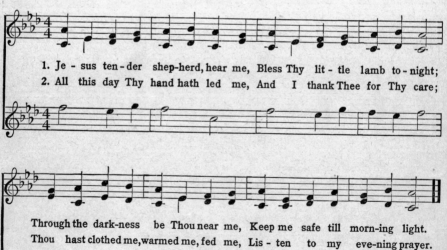

1. Je - sus ten - der shep-herd, hear me, Bless Thy lit - tle lamb to-night;
2. All this day Thy hand hath led me, And I thank Thee for Thy care;

Through the dark-ness be Thou near me, Keep me safe till morn-ing light.
Thou hast clothed me, warmed me, fed me, Lis - ten to my eve-ning prayer.

JOHN HENLEY

W. H. MONK

1. Chil - dren of Je - ru - sa - lem Sang the praise of Je - sus' Name;
2. We are taught to love the Lord We are taught to read His Word,
3. Par - ents, teach-ers, old and young, All u - nite to swell the song;

Chil - dren too of lat - ter days, Join to sing the Sav-iour's praise.
We are taught the way to heaven; Praise to God for all be given.
High - er yet and high - er rise, Till ho - san - nas reach the skies.

REFRAIN

Hark, Hark, Hark, while chil-dren's voic-es sing, Hark, Hark, Hark, while

chil-dren's voic - es sing, Loud ho - san - nas, Loud ho - san - nas,

Loud ho - san - nas to our King A - men A - men.

28 Who Are These Like Stars

REV. HEINRICH SCHENK
FRANCES COX, tr.

JOHN CHR. BACH

1. Who are these like stars ap-pear-ing, There, be-fore God's throne who stand? Each a gold-en crown is wear-ing: Who are all this glo-rious band? Hal-le-lu-jah, Prais-ing loud their heaven-ly King.

2. These are they who have con-tend-ed For their Sav-iour's hon-or long, Wrest-ling on till life was end-ed Fol-l'wing not the sin-ful throng; These who well the fight sus-tained, Tri-umph through the lamb have gained.

3. These like priests have watched and wait-ed, Of-f'ring up to Christ their will; Soul and bod-y con-se-crat-ed, Day and night they serve Him still; Now in God's most ho-ly place] Blest they stand be-fore His face.

There's a Friend for Little Children

ALBERT MIDLANE

SIR JOHN STAINER

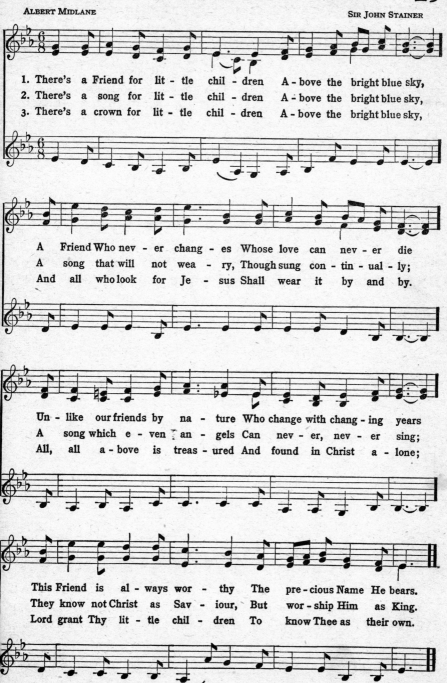

1. There's a Friend for lit - tle chil - dren A - bove the bright blue sky,
2. There's a song for lit - tle chil - dren A - bove the bright blue sky,
3. There's a crown for lit - tle chil - dren A - bove the bright blue sky,

A Friend Who nev - er chang - es Whose love can nev - er die
A song that will not wea - ry, Though sung con - tin - ual - ly;
And all who look for Je - sus Shall wear it by and by.

Un - like our friends by na - ture Who change with chang - ing years
A song which e - ven an - gels Can nev - er, nev - er sing;
All, all a - bove is treas - ured And found in Christ a - lone;

This Friend is al - ways wor - thy The pre - cious Name He bears.
They know not Christ as Sav - iour, But wor - ship Him as King.
Lord grant Thy lit - tle chil - dren To know Thee as their own.

30 Come Thou Fount

ROBERT ROBINSON

JOHN WYETH

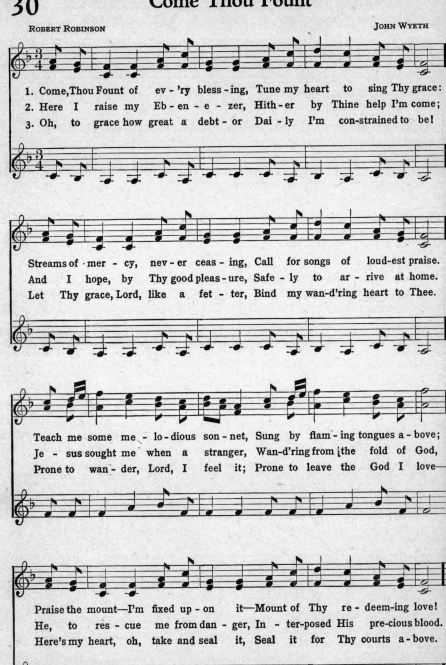

1. Come, Thou Fount of ev - 'ry bless - ing, Tune my heart to sing Thy grace:
2. Here I raise my Eb - en - e - zer, Hith - er by Thine help I'm come;
3. Oh, to grace how great a debt - or Dai - ly I'm con-strained to be!

Streams of mer - cy, nev - er ceas - ing, Call for songs of loud-est praise.
And I hope, by Thy good pleas - ure, Safe - ly to ar - rive at home.
Let Thy grace, Lord, like a fet - ter, Bind my wan-d'ring heart to Thee.

Teach me some me - lo - dious son - net, Sung by flam - ing tongues a - bove;
Je - sus sought me when a stranger, Wan-d'ring from the fold of God,
Prone to wan - der, Lord, I feel it; Prone to leave the God I love—

Praise the mount—I'm fixed up - on it—Mount of Thy re - deem-ing love!
He, to res - cue me from dan - ger, In - ter-posed His pre-cious blood.
Here's my heart, oh, take and seal it, Seal it for Thy courts a - bove.

Oh, Come

From German Choral

1. Oh, come, be glad and sing   To God our Lord and King!
2. Let praise to Him as - cend,   Whose glo - ry knows no end!

An - gel hosts re - joic - ing His glo - rious rule pro - claim,
Peace His king - dom's to - ken! Let all men Him a - dore,

Let men on earth be voic - ing The won - ders of His Name!
His reign shall be un - brok - en Who liv - eth ev - er - more.

Hon - or to Him bring,   Hon - or to Him bring.
Praise Him with - out end!   Praise Him with - out end.

32 All Glory, Laud and Honor

THEODULPH

MELCHOIR TECHNER

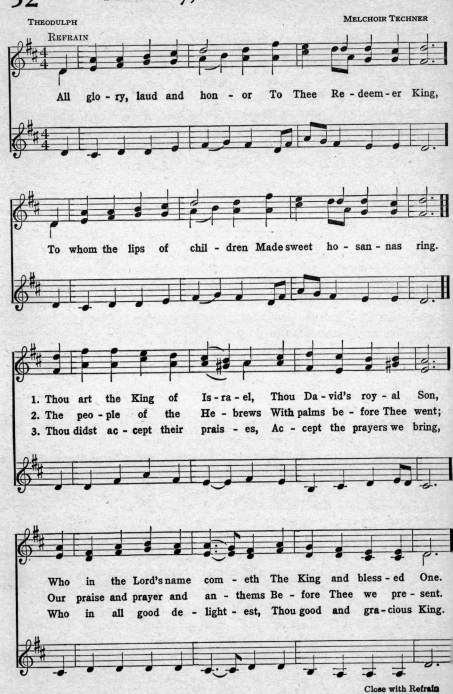

REFRAIN

All glo - ry, laud and hon - or To Thee Re - deem - er King,

To whom the lips of chil - dren Made sweet ho - san - nas ring.

1. Thou art the King of Is - ra - el, Thou Da - vid's roy - al Son,
2. The peo - ple of the He - brews With palms be - fore Thee went;
3. Thou didst ac - cept their prais - es, Ac - cept the prayers we bring,

Who in the Lord's name com - eth The King and bless - ed One.
Our praise and prayer and an - thems Be - fore Thee we pre - sent.
Who in all good de - light - est, Thou good and gra - cious King.

Close with Refrain

O God Our Father Thee We Praise

(LOBGESANG)

LEONARD CLOCK, 1590
Eng. Tr. J. C. WENGER

German Choral
Harmonized by W. E. YODER

1. O God, our Fa - ther Thee we praise, And laud Thy
Which Thou, O Lord so gra-cious-ly A - new hast

gra - cious bless - - ing. And hast led us to-
man - i - fest - - ed.

geth - er here, Lord to ad - mon - ish by Thy

word. Give us Thy grace to this end.

34   Faith of Our Fathers

FREDERICK W. FABER

J. G. WALTON

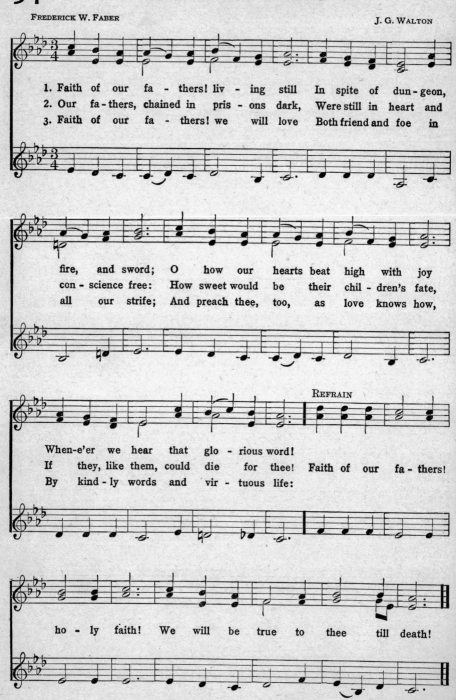

1. Faith of our fa - thers! liv - ing still In spite of dun - geon,
2. Our fa - thers, chained in pris - ons dark, Were still in heart and
3. Faith of our fa - thers! we will love Both friend and foe in

fire, and sword; O how our hearts beat high with joy
con - science free: How sweet would be their chil - dren's fate,
all our strife; And preach thee, too, as love knows how,

REFRAIN

When-e'er we hear that glo - rious word!
If they, like them, could die for thee! Faith of our fa - thers!
By kind - ly words and vir - tuous life:

ho - ly faith! We will be true to thee till death!

We Now Have Met to Worship Thee 35

J. S. SHOEMAKER

J. S. SHOEMAKER, 1889

1. We now have met to wor-ship Thee, And glo-ri-
   Help ev-'ry one at-ten-tive be, And heed the

2. As-sist Thy ser-vant to pro-claim The Gos-pel
   That all who hear ac-cept the same, And make in

fy Thy name, dear Lord;
teach-ing of Thy Word.   Fill ev-'ry heart with love di-vine,
mes-sage plain and pure,
Thee sal-va-tion sure.   In Thee a-lone help us to trust,

Teach ev-'ry tongue Thy praise to sing; Help each to say, Lord,
And in Thy love and laws a-bide, That when our bod-ies

we are Thine, And all we have to Thee we bring.
turn to dust, Our souls in heav'n be glo-ri-fied.

36   Be Careful of Your Thoughts

NAOMA STRUBHAR   GRACE BANKER

Be care-ful of your thoughts, dear, For they are great-er far

Than what is on the out-side, For as you think, you are.

Man looks on the out-er life He can see in part,

God looks on the in-ner life, He sees the heart.

I Know of a Stream

W. E. YODER Tr. from German

arr. W. E. YODER

1. I know of a stream with a glo - ri - ous power, Flows
2. The Stream is so deep and its wa - ter is clear, Its

won - drous-ly calm thru the land It spar - kles and gleams like a
fra - grance so love - ly and sweet; It heal - eth the sick, gives

flame of fire. Who knows this wa - ter of Life? O soul I
won -der-ful strength, Yes, mak - eth the poor sin - ner whole.

REFRAIN

bid you, Come: And seek this glo - ri - ous Stream Whose wa - ter flows

free and might - i - ly O be - lieve, it flow - eth for thee.

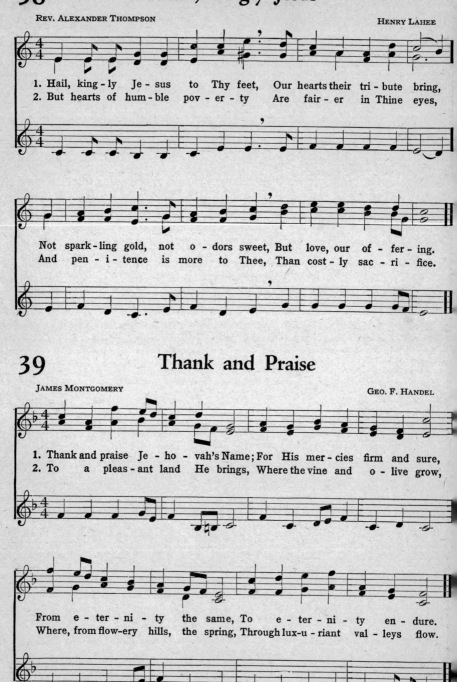

38 Hail, Kingly Jesus

REV. ALEXANDER THOMPSON

HENRY LAHEE

1. Hail, king-ly Je-sus to Thy feet, Our hearts their tri-bute bring,
2. But hearts of hum-ble pov-er-ty Are fair-er in Thine eyes,

Not spark-ling gold, not o-dors sweet, But love, our of-fer-ing.
And pen-i-tence is more to Thee, Than cost-ly sac-ri-fice.

39 Thank and Praise

JAMES MONTGOMERY

GEO. F. HANDEL

1. Thank and praise Je-ho-vah's Name; For His mer-cies firm and sure,
2. To a pleas-ant land He brings, Where the vine and o-live grow,

From e-ter-ni-ty the same, To e-ter-ni-ty en-dure.
Where, from flow-ery hills, the spring, Through lux-u-riant val-leys flow.

Come, Let Us Join Our Cheerful Song 40

ISAAC WATTS

GEORGE KINGSLEY

1. Come, let us join our cheer - ful song
2. "Wor - thy the Lamb that died," they cry,
3. The whole cre - a - tion join in one,

With an - gels round the throne; Ten thou - sand
"To be ex - alt - - ed thus", "Wor - thy the
To bless the sa - - cred name Of Him that

thou - sand are their tongues, But all their joys are
Lamb," our hearts re - ply, "For He was slain for
sits up - on the throne, And to a - dore the

one; But all their joys are one.
us For He was slain for us".
Lamb, And to a - dore the Lamb.

41 Watchman, What of the Night

JOHN BOWRING

LOWELL MASON
arr. WALTER E. YODER

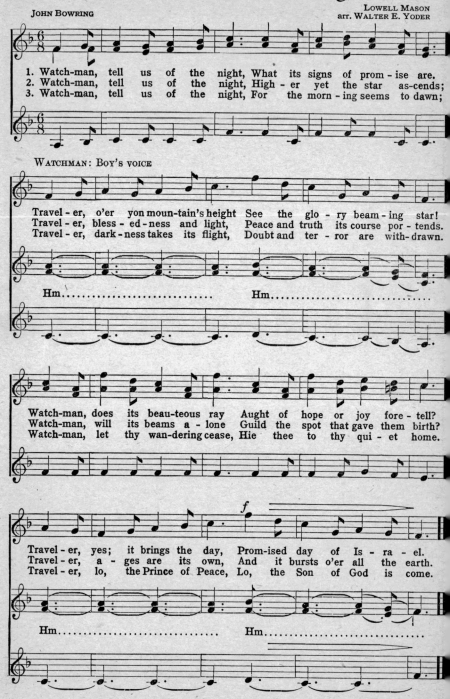

1. Watch-man, tell us of the night, What its signs of prom-ise are.
2. Watch-man, tell us of the night, High-er yet the star as-cends;
3. Watch-man, tell us of the night, For the morn-ing seems to dawn;

WATCHMAN: BOY'S VOICE

Travel-er, o'er yon moun-tain's height See the glo-ry beam-ing star!
Travel-er, bless-ed-ness and light, Peace and truth its course por-tends.
Travel-er, dark-ness takes its flight, Doubt and ter-ror are with-drawn.

Hm.................... Hm....................

Watch-man, does its beau-teous ray Aught of hope or joy fore-tell?
Watch-man, will its beams a-lone Guild the spot that gave them birth?
Watch-man, let thy wan-der-ing cease, Hie thee to thy qui-et home.

Travel-er, yes; it brings the day, Prom-ised day of Is-ra-el.
Travel-er, a-ges are its own, And it bursts o'er all the earth.
Travel-er, lo, the Prince of Peace, Lo, the Son of God is come.

Hm.................... Hm....................

A Child Is Born in Bethlehem

Unparthenisches Gesang Buch
Plain song Chant Tr. W. E. YODER

Harmonized by W. E. YODER

1. A child is born in Beth - le - hem, In
2. See here He lies in man - ger crib, In
3. The wise men came to greet their King, To
4. The Sav - iour came, rich grace He bore, Rich

Beth - le - hem. Let all re - joice Je - ru - sa - lem.
man - ger crib. His King - dom shall un - end - ing be.
greet their King. Brought gold and frank - in - cense and myrrh.
grace He bore, May God be praised for - ev - er more.

REFRAIN

Hal - le - lu - jah, Hal - le - lu - jah, Hal - le - lu - jah.

43 Silent Night

JOSEPH MOHR

FRANZ GRUBER

1. Si - lent night! Ho - ly night! All is calm,
2. Si - lent night! Ho - ly night! Shep - herds quake
3. Si - lent night! Ho - ly night! Son of God,

all is bright, Round yon vir - gin moth - er and Child;
at the sight! Glo - ries stream from heav - en a - far,
love's pnre light Ra - diant beams from Thy ho - ly face,

Ho - ly In - fant, so ten - der and mild,
Heav'n - ly hosts sing al - le - lu - ia. Sleep in
With the dawn of re - deem - ing grace,

heav - en - ly peace! Sleep in heav - en - ly peace.

THE BABE OF BETHLEHEM

The Angel's Hymn

JOHN W. WAYLAND

JOHN D. BRUNK

Allegro *f*

1. Fear not, fear not, O ye shep-herds, Rath-er give ye
2. For in yon-der town of Da-vid— Seek ye there with
3. This the sign by which to know Him, Seek ye, then, be

thanks and sing, For to you and to all peo-ple Ti-dings
one ac-cord— There is born to you a Sav-iour Which is
not a-fraid— Ye shall find a Babe in Beth-l'hem, In a

of great joy I bring.
e-ven Christ the Lord.
low-ly man-ger laid.

REFRAIN *p*

"Glo-ry in the high-est!

ff "Glo-ry, glo-ry in the high-est!

f

Praise in-crease, let praise in-crease! Glo-ry

Un-to God let praise in-crease!

glo-ry in the high-est! Un-to men good-will and peace."

45 Carol of the Shepherds

EDA LOU WALTON

Bohemian Carol

1. Come all ye shep-herds and be not dis-mayed,
2. Shep-herds have found Him in Beth-le-hem stall,

1. Come ye shep-herds, un-dis-mayed;
2. Shep-herds found Him in a stall,

Seek where the low-ly sweet ba-by is laid
Sing the glad ti-dings, oh sing them to all

Where the low-ly babe is laid.
Sing glad ti-dings sing to all!

Here in a man-ger far from all dan-ger Sleep-ing be-
Shep-herds a-dore Him Wise men be-fore Him Lay down their

hold Him Warm arms en-fold Him In Christ-mas cheer.
dow-er In glit-tering show-er Christ-mas is come.

'Tis Midnight
46

WM. BINGHAM TAPPAN

WM. B. BRADBURY

1. 'Tis mid-night, and on Ol - ive's brow The star is dimm'd that late - ly shone;
2. 'Tis mid-night, and from all re - moved The Sav-iour wres-tles 'lone with fears;
3. 'Tis mid-night, and for oth - er's guilt The Man of Sorrows weeps in blood;
4. 'Tis mid-night, and from eth - er plains Is borne the song that an - gels know;

'Tis mid-night in the gar - den now, The suf-f'ring Sav-iour prays a - lone.
E'en that dis - ci - ple whom He lov'd Heeds not His Master's grief and tears.
Yet he who hath in an - guish knelt, Is not for - sak-en by his God.
Un - heard by mor-tals are the strains That sweet-ly soothe the Sav-iour's woe.

When I Survey the Wondrous Cross
47

ISAAC WATTS

LOWELL MASON

1. When I sur-vey the won-drous cross On which the Prince of glo - ry died,
2. For - bid it, Lord, that I should boast, Save in the death of Christ my Lord;
3. See, from His head, His hands, His feet, Sor - row and love flow min-gled down;
4. Were the whole realm of na - ture mine, That were a pres - ent far too small;

My rich-est gain I count but loss, And pour con-tempt on all my pride.
All the vain things that charm me most, I sac - ri - fice to Je - sus' blood.
Did e'er such love and sor - row meet, Or thorns com-pose so rich a crown?
Love so a - maz - ing, so di - vine, De - mands my soul, my life, my all.

Bless Thou Our Gifts

Tune: Fling Wide the Portals, No. 111

Bless Thou the gifts our hands have brought;
    Bless Thou the work our hands have planned;
Ours is the faith, the will, the thought;
    The rest, O God, is in Thy hand, Amen.

Father, We Bring to Thee

Tune: Break Thou the Bread of Life

Father, we bring to Thee gifts of our love,
    Wilt thou accept them now as Thine above?
Thou hast so freely giv'n all that we need,
Our gifts and hearts and lives are Thine indeed. Amen.

Accept Our Offering

Tune: Bethany Blessings, No. 107

Accept our offering, Lord
    For all we have belongs to Thee.
O may it bring to others joy,
    May they Thy goodness see.
    For Jesus' sake. Amen!

ELIZABETH A. SHOWALTER

Offering Hymn

Tune: As With Gladness Men of Old

As they offered gifts most rare
At that manger rude and bare;
So may we, with holy joy,
Pure, and free from sin's alloy,
All our costliest treasures bring,
Christ, to Thee, our heavenly King. Amen.

WM. CHATTERTON DIX

There Is A Green Hill Far Away 48

Cecil F. Alexander

Geo. C. Stebbins
Arr. W. E. Yoder

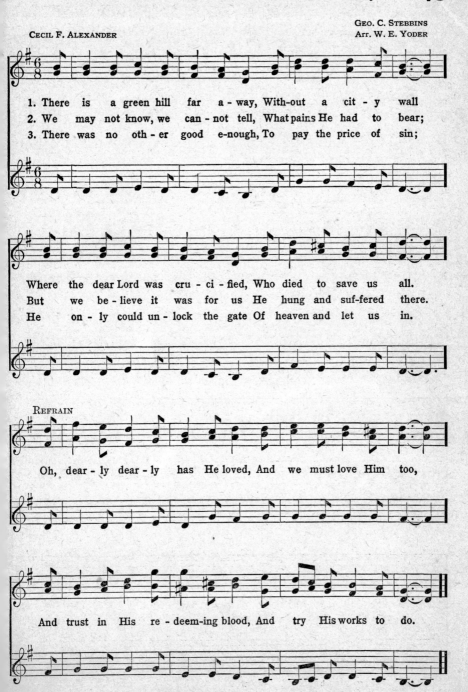

1. There is a green hill far a - way, With-out a cit - y wall
2. We may not know, we can - not tell, What pains He had to bear;
3. There was no oth - er good e-nough, To pay the price of sin;

Where the dear Lord was cru - ci - fied, Who died to save us all.
But we be - lieve it was for us He hung and suf-fered there.
He on - ly could un - lock the gate Of heaven and let us in.

REFRAIN

Oh, dear - ly dear - ly has He loved, And we must love Him too,

And trust in His re - deem-ing blood, And try His works to do.

49 Christ Is Risen

A. B. Kolb

A. B. Kolb

1. Christ who left His home in glo-ry, And up-on the cross was slain,
2. While the world in peace was sleep-ing, Ear-ly on that Eas-ter day,
3. Christ, our lov-ing Me-di-a-tor, Now with God for you and me

Now is ris'n! Oh, tell the sto-ry That the Sav-iour lives a-gain.
Came the faith-ful wo-men, weep-ing, But the stone was rolled a-way.
In-ter-ceds, and our Cre-a-tor Hears and an-swers ev-'ry plea.

REFRAIN

Hail Him! Hail Him! Tell the sto-ry;

Hail to the King, the might-y Redeemer! Hail Him who robbed the grave of its pow'r!

Hail all hail! Je-sus lives for-ev-er-more!
Tell ev-'ry na-tion all is well,

Tell ev-'ry na-tion all is well

THE RESURRECTION

Christ Is Risen

50

ALTO AND TENOR DUET

CHAUNCEY J. KING

1. Earth is bright, the li - lies sing, Christ is ris - en, Christ our
2. Birds are warb - ling on the wing, Christ is ris - en, Christ our
3. Sun-beams bright, the good news bring, Christ is ris - en, Christ our

King! In their sweet-ness hear them say, Je - sus Christ is ris-en to-day.
King! Peep-ing, twit-ter-ing, hear them say, Je - sus Christ is ris-en to-day.
King! Hark! and hear their joy - ful lay, Je - sus Christ is ris-en to-day.

CHORUS

Joy - ful - ly the Chil - dren sing, Christ is ris - en. Christ our King!

Hear them car - ol on their way, Je - sus Christ is ris-en to - day.

He Is Risen

51

Bible

Melody by MARY ROYER
Harmonized by WALTER E. YODER

rit.

He is not here For He is ris - en! For He is ris - en! as He said.

52 All the Happy Children

FRANCES DILLINGHAM

FRANCES R. HAVERGAL

1. All the hap-py chil-dren Glad-ly join our song,
2. See the sky a-bove us, Spreads so warm and blue;

Ris-ing to the Fa-ther, In a cho-rus strong.
So God's love is reach-ing O-ver me and you.

Birds are bright-ly sing-ing Leaves are open-ing wide,
Fa-ther dear, we thank Thee For long sum-mer days,

Flow-er bells are ring-ing Forth on ev-ery side.
For the birds and flow-ers For the grass-y ways.

All the hap-py chil-dren Glad-ly join our song,

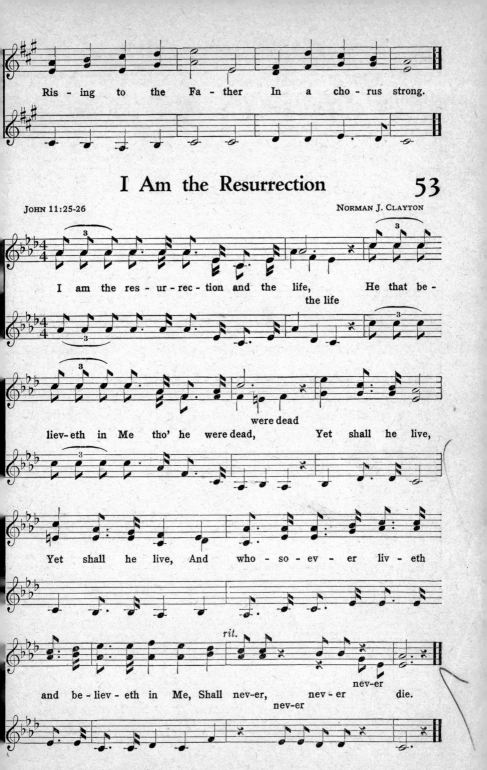

Ris - ing to the Fa - ther In a cho - rus strong.

I Am the Resurrection 53

John 11:25-26

Norman J. Clayton

I am the res - ur - rec - tion and the life, He that be -
the life

liev - eth in Me tho' he were dead, Yet shall he live,
were dead

Yet shall he live, And who - so - ev - er liv - eth

and be - liev - eth in Me, Shall nev - er, nev - er die.
nev-er nev-er

54 Around the Throne in Heaven

ANNA SHEPHERD

HENRY E. MATHEWS

1. A - round the throne of God in heaven Thou -
sands of chil - dren stand, Chil - dren whose sins are
all for - given, A ho - ly hap - py band sing - ing
Glo - ry Glo - ry Glo - ry be to God on high.

2. What brought them to the world a - bove, That
heaven so bright and fair; Where all is peace and
joy, and love, How came these chil - dren there sing - ing

3. On earth they sought the Sav - iour's grace On
earth they loved His Name; So now they see His
bless - ed face, And stand be - fore the Lamb, sing - ing

Hark, Ten Thousand Harps and Voices 55

THOMAS KELLEY LOWELL MASON

1. Hark, ten-thou-sand harps and voi-ces Sound the notes of praise a-bove;
2. King of glo-ry! reign for-ev-er—Thine an ev-er-last-ing crown;
3. Sav-iour! has-ten Thine ap-pear-ing; Bring, oh, bring the glo-rious day,

Je-sus reigns, and heav'n re-joic-es; Je-sus reigns, the God of love.
Noth-ing from Thy love, shall sev-er Those whom Thou hast made Thine own;
When, the aw-ful sum-mons hear-ing, Heav'n and earth shall pass a-way;—

See, He sits on yon-der throne; Je-sus rules the world a-lone.
Hap-py ob-jects of Thy grace Des-tined to be-hold Thy face.
Then, with golden harps we'll sing, "Glo-ry, glo-ry to our King!"

See, He sits on yon-der throne; Je-sus rules the world a-lone.
Hap-py ob-jects of Thy grace Destined to be-hold Thy face.
Then, with gold-en harps we'll sing, "Glo-ry, glo-ry to our King!"

Al-le-lu-ia, Al-le-lu-ia, Al-le-lu-ia! A-men.

56 Christ the Lord Cometh!

E. G. WESLEY

WILLIAM W. BENTLEY

1. Christ the Lord com-eth! per-chance at the dawn, Where earth a-
2. Christ the Lord com-eth! man know-eth not when, But when ye

wak-eth to wel-come the morn; Hath He not told us the
think not He com-eth a-gain; To all found watch-ing He

hour draw-eth near; Watch-ing and read-y His summons to hear?
bring-eth no fear, Nev-er a shad-ow, a part-ing a tear.

REFRAIN

Je-sus is com-ing we know not how soon, Com-ing at

mid-night, at morn-ing or noon; Eve-ning may bring Him to

bear us a - way;   For Him I'm watch-ing   and wait-ing each day.

Rejoice, the Lord Is King

57

CHARLES WESLEY

JOHN GOSS

1. Re - joice, the Lord is King: Your Lord and King   a - dore; Mor -
2. Je - sus, the Sav - iour, reigns,   The God of truth   and love; When
3. His king-dom can - not fail,   He rules o'er earth   and heav'n; The
4. He sits at God's right hand   Till all His foes   sub - mit, And

REFRAIN

tals, give thanks and sing,   And tri - umph ev - er - more:
He had purged our stains,   He took His seat a - bove: Lift up your
keys of death and hell   Are to our Je - sus giv'n:
bow to His com - mand,   And fall be-neath His feet:

heart, lift up your voice; Re - joice, a - gain   I say, re - joice.

58 I Chose a Star in Heaven

JOHN W. TUFT
arr. WALTER E. YODER

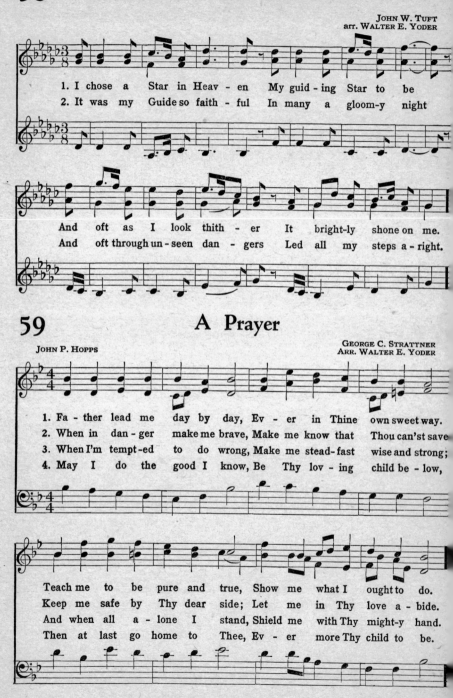

1. I chose a Star in Heav - en My guid - ing Star to be
2. It was my Guide so faith - ful In many a gloom - y night

And oft as I look thith - er It bright - ly shone on me.
And oft through un - seen dan - gers Led all my steps a - right.

59 A Prayer

JOHN P. HOPPS

GEORGE C. STRATTNER
ARR. WALTER E. YODER

1. Fa - ther lead me day by day, Ev - er in Thine own sweet way.
2. When in dan - ger make me brave, Make me know that Thou can'st save
3. When I'm tempt - ed to do wrong, Make me stead - fast wise and strong;
4. May I do the good I know, Be Thy lov - ing child be - low,

Teach me to be pure and true, Show me what I ought to do.
Keep me safe by Thy dear side; Let me in Thy love a - bide.
And when all a - lone I stand, Shield me with Thy might - y hand.
Then at last go home to Thee, Ev - er more Thy child to be.

Take Time to Be Holy

W. D. Longstaff

Geo. C. Stebbins

1. Take time to be ho - ly, Speak oft with thy Lord;
2. Take time to be ho - ly, The world rush - es on;
3. Take time to be ho - ly, Let Him be thy Guide,
4. Take time to be ho - ly, Be calm in thy soul;

A - bide in Him al - ways, And feed on His word;
Spend much time in se - cret With Je - sus a - lone;
And run not be - fore Him, What - ev - er be - tide;
Each thought and each mo - tive Be - neath His con - trol;

Make friends of God's chil - dren, Help those who are weak,
By look - ing to Je - sus, Like Him thou shalt be;
In joy or in sor - row, Still fol - low thy Lord,
Thus led by His spir - it To foun - tains of love,

For - get - ing in noth - ing His bless - ing to seek.
Thy friends in thy con - duct His like - ness shall see.
And, look - ing to Je - sus, Still trust in His Word.
Thou soon shall be fit - ted For ser - vice a - bove.

61 Walk in the Light

BERNARD BARTON

F. JOSEPH HAYDN
Arr. WALTER E. YODER

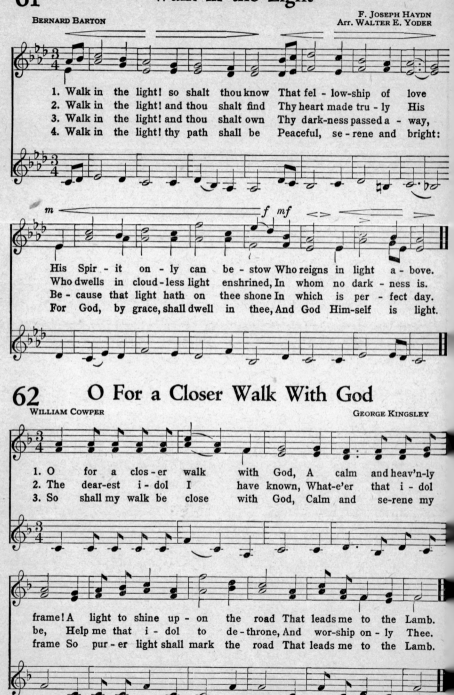

1. Walk in the light! so shalt thou know That fel - low-ship of love
2. Walk in the light! and thou shalt find Thy heart made tru - ly His
3. Walk in the light! and thou shalt own Thy dark-ness passed a - way,
4. Walk in the light! thy path shall be Peaceful, se - rene and bright:

His Spir - it on - ly can be - stow Who reigns in light a - bove.
Who dwells in cloud - less light enshrined, In whom no dark - ness is.
Be - cause that light hath on thee shone In which is per - fect day.
For God, by grace, shall dwell in thee, And God Him-self is light.

62 O For a Closer Walk With God

WILLIAM COWPER

GEORGE KINGSLEY

1. O for a clos - er walk with God, A calm and heav'n-ly
2. The dear-est i - dol I have known, What-e'er that i - dol
3. So shall my walk be close with God, Calm and se - rene my

frame! A light to shine up - on the road That leads me to the Lamb.
be, Help me that i - dol to de - throne, And wor-ship on - ly Thee.
frame So pur - er light shall mark the road That leads me to the Lamb.

Dear Lord and Father of Mankind

JOHN G. WHITTIER

FREDERICK C. MAKER

63

1. Dear Lord and Fa - ther of man - kind, For-
2. In sim - ple trust like theirs who heard, Be-
3. O Sab - bath rest by Gal - i - lee! O
4. Drop Thy still dews of qui - et - ness, Till
5. Breathe thro' the heats of our de - sire Thy

give our fool - ish ways; Re - clothe us in our
side the Syr - ian sea, The gra - cious call - ing
calm of hills a - bove, Where Je - sus knelt to
all our striv - ings cease; Take from our souls the
cool - ness and Thy balm; Let sense be dumb, let

right - ful mind, In pur - er lives Thy
of the Lord, Let us, like them, with -
share with Thee The si - lence of e -
strain and stress, And let our or - dered
flesh re - tire; Speak thro' the earth - quake

serv - ice find, In deep - er rev - 'rence, praise.
out a word Rise up and fol - low Thee.
ter - ni - ty In - ter - pret - ed by love!
lives con - fess The beau - ty of Thy peace.
wind and fire, O still, small voice of calm. A - men.

64 God Speed the Right

H. E. HICKSON

German Folk Melody

1. Now to heav'n our prayer as-cend-ing God speed the right;
2. Be that prayer a-gain re-peat-ed, God speed the right;
3. Still our on-ward course pur-su-ing, God speed the right;

In our no-ble cause con-tend-ing God speed the right;
Ne'er des-pair-ing though de-feat-ed; God speed the right;
Ev-ery foe at length sub-du-ing, God speed the right;

Be our zeal in heav'n re-cord-ed; With suc-cess on earth re-
Like the good and great in sto-ry, If we fail we fail in
Truth our cause, what-e'er de-lay it, There's no power on earth to

ward-ed God speed the right, God speed the right.
glo-ry, God speed the right, God speed the right.
stay it, God speed the right, God speed the right.

Life's Highest Motto

(OTHERS)

C. D. MEIGS

WALTER E. YODER

65

1. Lord help me live from day to day, In such a self-for-
2. Help me in all the work I do, To ev-er be sin-

get-ful way That ev-en when I kneel to pray, My
cere and true And know that all I'd do for you, Must

pray'r shall be for Oth-ers.
needs be done for Oth-ers.

REFRAIN

Oth-ers Lord, yes
Oth-ers, And less of self for me, Help
me to live for Oth-ers That I may live like Thee.

rit. p

66 Does Jesus Care

Rev. Frank E. Graff

J. Lincoln Hall

1. Does Je-sus care When my heart is pained Too deep-ly for mirth or song;
2. Does Je-sus care When my way is dark With a nameless dread and fear?

Hum..........Hum....................Hum....................

As the burdens press And the cares dis-tress, And the way grows weary and long.
As the day-light fades Into deep night shades, Does He care e-nough to be near.

Hum....................Hum................Hum....................

REFRAIN

Oh, yes, He cares I know He cares; His heart is touched with my grief;

When the days are wea-ry, the long nights dreary I know my Sav-iour cares.

(He cares)

I Owe the Lord a Morning Song

(GRATITUDE)

Amos Herr   Amos Herr

1. I owe the Lord a morn - ing song Of
2. He kept me safe an - oth - er night; I
3. Keep me from dan - ger and from sin; Help
4. Keep me till Thou wilt call me hence, Where

grat - i - tude and praise, For the kind mer - cy
see an - oth - er day; Now may His Spir - it
me Thy will to do, So that my heart be
nev - er night can be; And save me, Lord, for

He has shown In length - 'ning out my days.
as the light, Di - rect me in His way.
pure with - in; And I Thy good - ness know.
Je - sus' sake,— He shed His blood for me.

68 Saviour, Like a Shepherd Lead Us

Mary A. S. Barber   Wm. B. Bradbury

1. Sav - iour, like a shep-herd lead us, Much we need Thy tend'rest care;
2. We are Thine, do Thou be - friend us, Be the guard-ian of our way;
3. Thou hast promised to re - ceive us, Poor and sin - ful tho' we be;
4. Ear - ly let us seek Thy fa - vor, Ear - ly let us do Thy will;

In Thy pleas-ant pas-tures feed us, For our use Thy folds pre-pare;
Keep Thy flock, from sin de - fend us, Seek us when we go a - stray;
Thou hast mer - cy to re - lieve us, Grace to cleanse, and pow'r to free:
Bless - ed Lord and on - ly Sav - iour, With Thy love our bos-oms fill:

Bless - ed Je - sus! Bless-ed Je - sus! Thou hast bought us, Thine we are,
Bless - ed Je - sus! Bless-ed Je - sus! Hear, O hear us, when we pray,
Blees - ed Je - sus! Bless-ed Je - sus! We will ear - ly turn to Thee,
Bless - ed Je - sus! Bless-ed Je - sus! Thou hast loved us, love us still,

Bless-ed Je - sus! Bless-ed Je - sus! Thou hast bought us, Thine we are.
Bless - ed Je - sus! Bless-ed Je - sus! Hear, O hear us, when we pray.
Bless-ed Je - sus! Bless-ed Je - sus! We will ear - ly turn to Thee.
Bless-ed Je - sus! Bless-ed Je - sus! Thou hast loved us, love us still.

THE GOOD SHEPHERD

God Be With You

(Without refrain)

God be with you till we meet again,
By His counsels guide, uphold you,
With His sheep securely fold you,
God be with you till we meet again. Amen.

JEREMIAH E. RANKIN

Ere We Part

Tune: Hymn of Joy, No. 101

Ere we part, O God our Father,
To each heart Thy blessing give;
And may we, Thy grace possessing,
Ever to Thy glory live. Amen.

RICHARD HUMPHREY

Heavenly Father, Bless Us

Tune: Now the Day is Over, No. 10

Heav'nly Father, bless us; Jesus, be our Friend;
Holy Spirit, guide us to our journey's end.

The Lord Bless Thee

NUMBERS 6:24-26

NETTIE D. ELLSWORTH
Arr. W. E. YODER

The Lord bless thee, and keep thee; The Lord make His face shine up-

on thee and give thee peace, and give thee peace. A - men A - men.

69 He Cares for Me

"Norse Lullaby"
Arr. W. E. YODER

1. How strong and sweet my Fa - ther's care, That round a - bout me like the air, Is with me al - ways ev - ery - where, Is with me al - ways, ev - ery - where! He cares for me.

2. Oh, keep me ev - er in Thy love, Dear Fa - ther watch - ing from a - bove, And let me still Thy mer - cy prove. And let me still Thy mer - cy prove, And care for me.

Follow the Path of Jesus

(BOUND BROOK)

From Hymns and Tunes

1. Fol - low the path to Je - sus, Walk where His foot-steps lead;
2. Cling to the hand of Je - sus, All thru the day and night;

Keep in His beam - ing pres - ence, Ev - 'ry coun - sel heed;
Dark though the way and drear - y, He will guide you right.

Watch, while the hours are fly - ing, Read - y some good to do;
Live for [the good of oth - ers, Help- less, op-pressed and wrong;

Quick, while His voice is call - ing Yield o - be - dience true!
Lift them from depths of sor - row, In His strength be strong!

71 Yield Not to Temptation

H. R. Palmer
H. R. Palmer

1. Yield not to temp - ta - tion, For yield - ing is sin;
2. Shun e - vil com - pan - ions, Bad lan - guage dis - dain,

Each vic - t'ry will help you Some oth - er to win;
God's name hold in rev - 'rence Nor take it in vain;

Fight man - ful - ly on - ward, Dark pas - sions sub - due
Be thought-ful and ear - nest, Kind heart - ed and true

Look ev - er to Je - sus He'll car - ry you through.

REFRAIN

Ask the Sav - iour to help you, Com - fort strengthen and keep you;

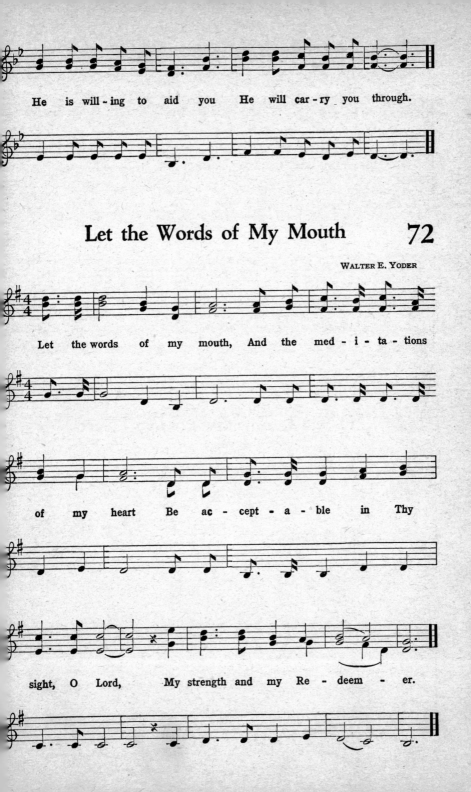

He is will-ing to aid you He will car-ry you through.

Let the Words of My Mouth 72

WALTER E. YODER

Let the words of my mouth, And the med - i - ta - tions

of my heart Be ac - cept - a - ble in Thy

sight, O Lord, My strength and my Re - deem - er.

73 Children of the Heavenly Father

Tryggare Kan ingen vara

Swedish Folksong

1. Chil - dren of the heav'n-ly Fa - ther Safe-ly in His bos-om gath-er, Nes-tling
2. Praise the Lord in joy - ful num-bers: Your Pro-tect-ors nev-er slumbers: At the
3. Though He giv - eth or He tak - eth, God His chil-dren ne'er for-sak-eth, His the

bird nor star in heav - en Such a ref - uge e'er was giv - en.
will of your De-fend - er Ev - ery foe - man must sur - ren - der.
lov - ing pur-pose sole - ly To pre-serve them pure and ho - ly. A - men.

74 O Master of the Loving Heart
(SERENITY)

CALVIN W. LAUFER, 1926

WILLIAM V. WALLACE

1. O Mas - ter of the lov - ing heart, The Friend of all in need,
2. O grant us hearts like Thine, dear Lord, So joy - ous, true, and free,

We pray that we may be like Thee In thought and word and deed.
That all Thy chil-dren ev - ery-where Be drawn by us to Thee.

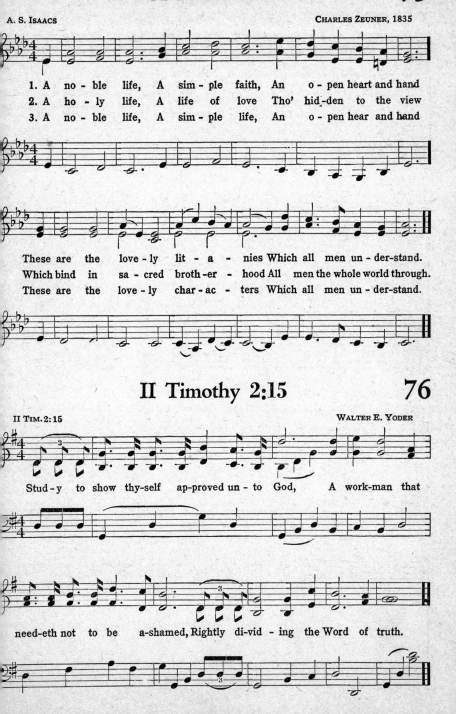

A Noble Life

A. S. ISAACS

CHARLES ZEUNER, 1835

1. A no - ble life, A sim - ple faith, An o - pen heart and hand
2. A ho - ly life, A life of love Tho' hid-den to the view
3. A no - ble life, A sim - ple life, An o - pen hear and hand

These are the love - ly lit - a - nies Which all men un - der-stand.
Which bind in sa - cred broth - er - hood All men the whole world through.
These are the love - ly char - ac - ters Which all men un - der-stand.

II Timothy 2:15

II TIM. 2:15

WALTER E. YODER

Stud - y to show thy-self ap-proved un - to God, A work-man that

need-eth not to be a-shamed, Rightly di-vid - ing the Word of truth.

77   Lord I Want to be a Christian

Spiritual

1. Lord I want to be a Chris-tian,
2. Lord I want to be more lov-ing, In - a my heart, in - a my heart
3. Lord I want to be like Je - sus,

Lord I want to be a Chris - tian,
Lord I want to be more lov - ing, In - a my heart.
Lord I want to be like Je - sus,

In - a my heart, In - a my heart, In - a my heart, In - a my heart

Lord, I want to be a Chris - tian,
Lord, I want to be more lov - ing, In - a my heart.
Lord, I want to be like Je - sus,

Somebody

J. R. CLEMENTS

W. S. WEEDEN

1. Some-bod-y did a gold-en deed, Prov-ing him-
2. Some-bod-y filled the day with light, Con-stant-ly

self a friend in-deed; Some-bod-y sang a cheer-ful
chased a-way the night; Some-bod-y's work bore joy and

song, Bright-ning the sky the whole day long,
peace, Sure-ly his life shall nev-er cease,

Was that some-bod-y you? Was that some-bod-y you?

79 By Cool Siloam's Shady Rill

R. Heber

Johannas Brahms

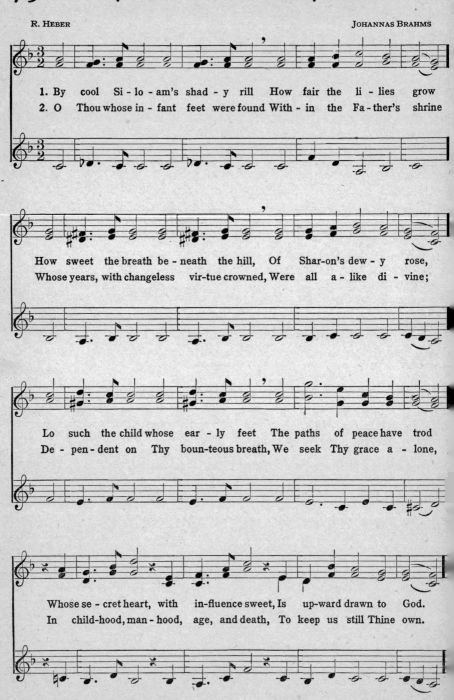

1. By cool Si-lo-am's shad-y rill How fair the li-lies grow
2. O Thou whose in-fant feet were found With-in the Fa-ther's shrine

How sweet the breath be-neath the hill, Of Shar-on's dew-y rose,
Whose years, with changeless vir-tue crowned, Were all a-like di-vine;

Lo such the child whose ear-ly feet The paths of peace have trod
De-pen-dent on Thy boun-teous breath, We seek Thy grace a-lone,

Whose se-cret heart, with in-fluence sweet, Is up-ward drawn to God.
In child-hood, man-hood, age, and death, To keep us still Thine own.

Prayer Is the Soul's Sincere Desire

80

JAMES MONTGOMERY

THOMAS HASTINGS

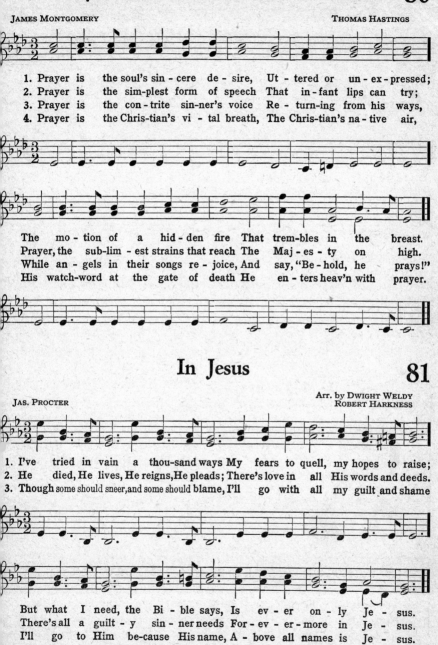

1. Prayer is the soul's sin - cere de - sire, Ut - tered or un - ex - pressed;
2. Prayer is the sim-plest form of speech That in - fant lips can try;
3. Prayer is the con - trite sin - ner's voice Re - turn-ing from his ways,
4. Prayer is the Chris-tian's vi - tal breath, The Chris-tian's na - tive air,

The mo - tion of a hid - den fire That trem-bles in the breast.
Prayer, the sub-lim - est strains that reach The Maj - es - ty on high.
While an - gels in their songs re - joice, And say, "Be - hold, he prays!"
His watch-word at the gate of death He en - ters heav'n with prayer.

In Jesus

81

JAS. PROCTER

Arr. by DWIGHT WELDY
ROBERT HARKNESS

1. I've tried in vain a thou-sand ways My fears to quell, my hopes to raise;
2. He died, He lives, He reigns, He pleads; There's love in all His words and deeds.
3. Though some should sneer, and some should blame, I'll go with all my guilt and shame

But what I need, the Bi - ble says, Is ev - er on - ly Je - sus.
There's all a guilt - y sin - ner needs For - ev - er-more in Je - sus.
I'll go to Him be-cause His name, A - bove all names is Je - sus.

82 I Think When I Read

JEMIMA THOMPSON LUKE

1. I think when I read that sweet sto - ry of old,
2. I wish that His hands had been placed on my head,
3. Yet still to His foot - stool in prayer I may go,

When Je - sus was here a - mong men,
That His arm had been thrown a - round me
And ask for a share of His love;

How He called lit - tle chil - dren as lambs to His fold,
And that I might of seen His kind look when He said,
And if I now ear - nest - ly seek Him be - low,

molto rit.

I should like to have been with Him then.
"Let the lit - tle ones come un - to me."
I shall hear Him and see Him a - bove.

And Can It Be

JEREMIAH INGALLS
arr. WALTER E. YODER

CHARLES WESLEY

1. And can it be that I should gain, An in-terest in the
2. 'Tis mys-tery all, Th'Im-mor-tal dies, Who can ex-plore His
3. No con-dem-na-tion now I dread, Je-sus, with all in

Sav-iour's blood? Died He for me, who caused His pain? For
strange de-sign? In vain the first born ser-aph tries To
Him, is mine; A-live in Him my liv-ing head, And

me, who Him to death pur-sued? A-maz-ing love!
sound the depth of love di-vine; 'Tis mer-cy all,
clothed in right-eous-ness di-vine, Bold I ap-proach

how can it be That Thou, my Lord, shouldst die for me.
let all a-dore; Let an-gel minds in-quire no more.
th'e-ter-nal throne, And claim the crown, through Christ, my own.

84 What a Friend We Have in Jesus

JOSEPH SCRIVEN

CHARLES C. CONVERSE

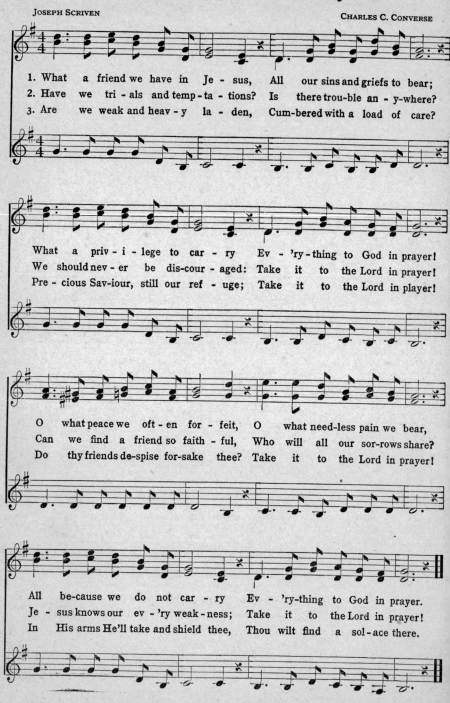

1. What a friend we have in Je - sus, All our sins and griefs to bear;
2. Have we tri - als and temp - ta - tions? Is there trou-ble an - y-where?
3. Are we weak and heav - y la - den, Cum-bered with a load of care?

What a priv - i - lege to car - ry Ev - 'ry-thing to God in prayer!
We should nev - er be dis-cour - aged: Take it to the Lord in prayer!
Pre - cious Sav-iour, still our ref - uge; Take it to the Lord in player!

O what peace we oft - en for - feit, O what need-less pain we bear,
Can we find a friend so faith - ful, Who will all our sor-rows share?
Do thy friends de-spise for-sake thee? Take it to the Lord in prayer!

All be-cause we do not car - ry Ev - 'ry-thing to God in prayer.
Je - sus knows our ev - 'ry weak - ness; Take it to the Lord in prayer!
In His arms He'll take and shield thee, Thou wilt find a sol - ace there.

O Come to My Heart

85

EMILY ELLIOTT

T. R. MATHEWS

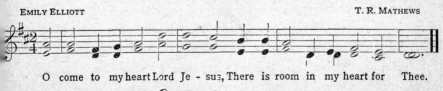

O come to my heart Lord Je - sus, There is room in my heart for Thee.

86 Jesus Loves Us All

IRENE E. WITMER

IRENE E. WITMER

1. Je - sus loves the lit - tle chil - dren, Loves them with a ten-der love
2. We are Je - sus' lit - tle chil - dren, And how hap - py we should be

While on earth to them He ren - dered, Deeds of kind - ness, words of love.
That al-though He's now in Heav - en, He loves ev - en you and me.

Suf - fer the chil - dren to come un - to me, Suf - fer the

chil - dren to come un - to me And for - bid them

not for such is the king - dom of heaven.

Jesus Loves Me

ANNA BARTLETT WARNER

WILLIAM B. BRADBURY

1. Je - sus loves me! this I know, For the Bi - ble tells me so;
2. Je - sus loves me! He who died, Heav-en's gate to o - pen wide;
3. Je - sus loves me! loves me still, Though I'm ver - y weak and ill;
4. Je - sus loves me! He will stay Close be - side me all the way;

Lit - tle ones to Him be - long; They are weak, but He is strong.
He will wash a - way my sin, Let His lit - tle child come in.
From His shin - ing throne on high, Comes to watch me where I lie.
If I love Him, when I die He will take me home on high.

REFRAIN

Yes, Je - sus loves me, Yes, Je - sus loves me,

Yes, Je - sus loves me— The Bi - ble tells me so.

88 I Love to Hear the Story

MRS. EMILY MILLER

GEO. F. ROOT

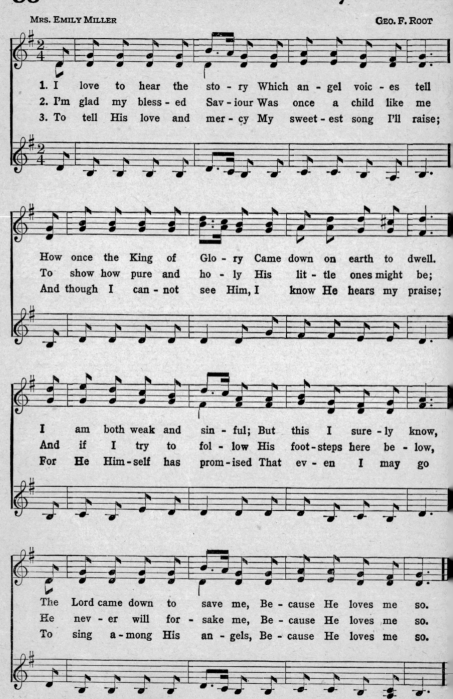

1. I love to hear the sto-ry Which an-gel voic-es tell
2. I'm glad my bless-ed Sav-iour Was once a child like me
3. To tell His love and mer-cy My sweet-est song I'll raise;

How once the King of Glo-ry Came down on earth to dwell.
To show how pure and ho-ly His lit-tle ones might be;
And though I can-not see Him, I know He hears my praise;

I am both weak and sin-ful; But this I sure-ly know,
And if I try to fol-low His foot-steps here be-low,
For He Him-self has prom-ised That ev-en I may go

The Lord came down to save me, Be-cause He loves me so.
He nev-er will for-sake me, Be-cause He loves me so.
To sing a-mong His an-gels, Be-cause He loves me so.

Seek Ye the Lord

WALTER E. YODER

Seek ye the Lord, While He may be found;

Seek ye the Lord While He may be found.

Call ye up-on Him While He is near, While He is near.

90 Just As I Am Thine Own to Be

MARIANNE HEARN

JOSEPH BARNBY

1. Just as I am, Thine own to be Friend of the
2. In the glad morn - ing of my day, My life to

young, Who lov - est me, To con - se - crate my-
give, My vows to pay, With no re - serve and

self to Thee, O Je - sus Christ, I come.
no de - lay, With all my heart I come. A - men.

I Would Be True

Howard A. Walter

Joseph Y. Peek

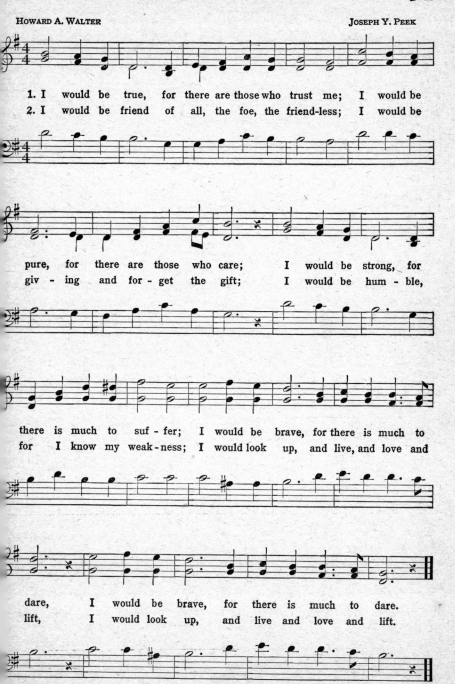

1. I would be true, for there are those who trust me; I would be
2. I would be friend of all, the foe, the friend-less; I would be

pure, for there are those who care; I would be strong, for
giv - ing and for - get the gift; I would be hum - ble,

there is much to suf - fer; I would be brave, for there is much to
for I know my weak - ness; I would look up, and live, and love and

dare, I would be brave, for there is much to dare.
lift, I would look up, and live and love and lift.

92 Let There Be Light

WILLIAM VORIES

WILLIAM BOYD
Arr. WALTER E. YODER

1. Let there be light, Lord God of Hosts; Let there be
2. With-in our pass-ioned hearts in-still The calm that
3. Give us the peace of vi - sion clear To see our
4. Let woe and waste of war-fare cease, That use-ful

wis - dom on the earth! Let broad hu - man - i -
end - eth strain and strife; Make us Thy min - is -
broth - ers' good our own, To joy and suf - fer
la - bor yet may build Its homes with love and

ty have birth; Let there be deeds in - stead of boasts.
ters of life; Purge us from lusts that curse and kill.
not a - lone; The love that cast - eth out all fear.
vir - tue filled. God give Thy way - ward chil - dren peace.

Cast Thy Burden Upon the Lord

From "ELIJAH"

FELIX MENDELSSOHN

Cast thy bur-den up-on the Lord; And He shall sus-

tain thee; He nev-er will suf-fer the right-eous to fall,

He is at thy right hand. Thy mer-cy Lord is

great And far a-bove the heavens Let none be

made a-sham-ed That wait up-on Thee.

94 The Beatitudes

MATHEW 5

WALTER E. YODER, 1942

SOLO , CHORUS

Bless - ed are the poor in spir - it: for theirs is the king-dom of heaven.

Bless - ed are they that mourn: for they shall be com - fort - ed.

Bless - ed are the meek: for they shall in - her - it the earth.

Bless - ed are they which do hun - ger and thirst af - ter righteousness; for

they shall be fill - ed. Bless - ed are the mer - ci - ful: for

they shall ob - tain mer - cy. Bless - ed are the pure in heart: for

they shall see God. Bless - ed are the peace-mak - ers: for they shall be

call'd the chil-dren of God. Bless - ed are they which are per - se - cut-ed for

right - eous-ness sake: for theirs is the king-dom of heaven. Bless - ed are

ye when men re - vile and per - se - cute you and shall say all man-ner of

e - vil a-gainst you false - ly for my sake. Re-joice and be ex - ceed-ing

glad for great is your re-ward in heaven. A - men A - men.

95 The Great Commission

Matthew 28:18, 19, 20

Walter E. Yoder

All power is given un-to Me in heav'n and in earth; Go ye

there-fore and teach all na-tions, bap-tiz-ing them in the

Name of the Fa-ther and of the Son, And of the Ho-ly

Ghost. Teach-ing them to ob-serve all things What-so-ev-er

I've com-mand-ed you; And lo, I am with you

al-way, e-ven un-to the end of the world. A-men A-men.

For the Beauty of the Earth 96

FOLLIOTT S. PIERPOINT

CONRAD KOCHER
Arr. W. E. YODER

1. For the beau - ty of the earth, For the beau - ty of the skies,
2. For the joy of hu - man love, Broth - er, sis - ter, par - ent, child,
3. For Thy Church, that ev - er - more Lift - eth ho - ly hands a - bove,
4. For Thy-self, best gift di - vine, To our race so free - ly giv'n;

For the love which from our birth O - ver and a - round us lies,—
Friends on earth, and friends a - bove; For all gen - tle thoughts and mild,—
Of - f'ring up on ev - 'ry shore Its pure sac - ri - fice of love,—
For that great, great love of Thine, Peace on earth, and joy in heav'n,—

Christ our God, to Thee we raise This our hymn of grate - ful praise.

The Lord Is in His Holy Temple 97

HABAKKUK 2:20

E. O. EXCELL
Arr. W. E. YODER

The Lord is in His ho - ly tem - ple: Let all the earth keep

si - lence, keep si - lence be - fore Him. A - men.

98 My Faith Looks Up to Thee

RAY PALMER

LOWELL MASON
Arr. W. E. Yoder

1. My faith looks up to Thee, Thou Lamb of Cal - va - ry, Sav - iour di - vine! Now hear me while I pray, Take all my guilt a - way; Oh, let me from this day Be whol - ly Thine!

2. May Thy rich' grace im - part Strength to my faint - ing heart, My zeal in - spire; As Thou hast died for me Oh, may my love to Thee Pure, warm, and change - less be, A liv - ing fire!

3. While life's dark maze I tread, And griefs a - round me spread, Be Thou my guide, Bid dark - ness turn to day, Wipe sor - row's tears a - way, Nor let me ev - er stray From Thee a - side.

4. When ends life's tran - sient dream, When death's cold sul - len stream Shall o'er me roll, Blest Sav - iour, then, in love Fear and dis - trust re - move; Oh, bear me safe a - bove, A ran - somed soul!

Ask, Seek, Knock

MATT. 7:7

BENJ. A. BAUER
Arr. W. E. YODER

Ask, and it shall be giv - en you; Seek, and ye shall find;

Knock, and it shall be o - pened un - to you.

Ask, and it shall be giv - en you; Seek, and ye shall find;

Knock, and it shall be o - pened un - to you.

100 Saviour, Hear Us, We Pray

W. W. Ellsworth

Johannes Brahms
Arr. W. E. Yoder

1. Sav-iour, hear us, we pray, Keep us safe thro' this day; Keep our lives
2. Be our Guard-ian and Guide; May we walk by Thy side Till the eve-

free from sin, And our hearts pure with-in. Je-sus Lord, hear our prayer,
ning shades fall O-ver us, o-ver us.

Refrain

May we rest in Thy care; Je-sus Lord, hear our prayer, May we rest in Thy care.

101 Hymns of Thanks

Ludwig Van Beethoven
Arr. W. E. Yoder

Lord of ev-ery land and na-tion, Thou hast blest us won-drous-ly;

For our growth and pres-er-va-tion, Heart-y thanks we give to Thee.

From *The Music Hour*, Third Book, Copyright 1929, by special permission of the publishers, The Silver Burdett Co., New York.

Bless the Lord

Ps. 103

H. D. Weaver
Arr. by W. E. Yoder

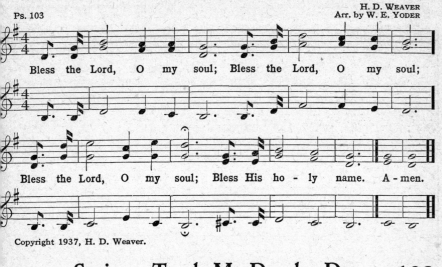

Bless the Lord, O my soul; Bless the Lord, O my soul;

Bless the Lord, O my soul; Bless His ho - ly name. A - men.

Copyright 1937, H. D. Weaver.

Saviour, Teach Me Day by Day

JANE E. LEESON

Arr. W. E. YODER

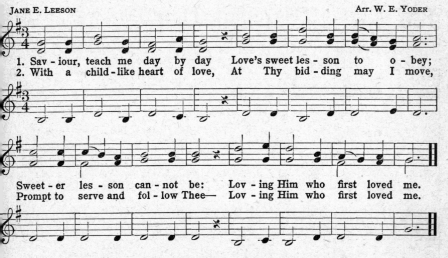

1. Sav - iour, teach me day by day Love's sweet les - son to o - bey;
2. With a child - like heart of love, At Thy bid - ding may I move,

Sweet - er les - son can - not be: Lov - ing Him who first loved me.
Prompt to serve and fol - low Thee— Lov - ing Him who first loved me.

Father, Bless Our School Today

Tune: Saviour, Teach Me Day by Day

Father, bless our school today;
Be in all we do or say;
Be in ev'ry song we sing,
Ev'ry prayer to Thee we bring.

Jesus, well beloved Son,
May Thy will by us be done,
Come and meet with us today;
Teach us, Lord, Thyself, we pray.

Holy Spirit, mighty Pow'r,
Grace and blessings on us show'r,
Unto us Thy unction give;
Touch our souls that we may live.

Holy Father, holy Son,
Holy Spirit, Three in One!
Glory as of old to Thee
Now and evermore shall be.

Anon.

105 The Lord Be with Us

John Ellerton

John B. Dykes
Arr. W. E. Yoder

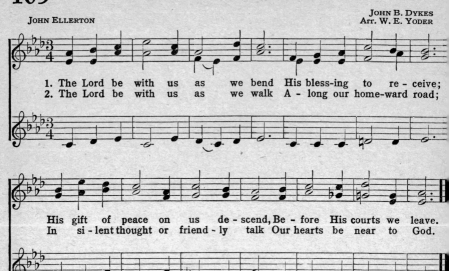

1. The Lord be with us as we bend His bless-ing to re-ceive;
2. The Lord be with us as we walk A-long our home-ward road;

His gift of peace on us de-scend, Be-fore His courts we leave.
In si-lent thought or friend-ly talk Our hearts be near to God.

106 Holy Spirit, Hear Us

William H. Parker

John C. H. Rink
Arr. Walter E. Yoder

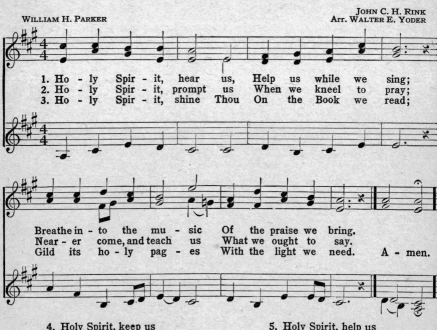

1. Ho-ly Spir-it, hear us, Help us while we sing;
2. Ho-ly Spir-it, prompt us When we kneel to pray;
3. Ho-ly Spir-it, shine Thou On the Book we read;

Breathe in-to the mu-sic Of the praise we bring.
Near-er come, and teach us What we ought to say.
Gild its ho-ly pag-es With the light we need.   A-men.

4. Holy Spirit, keep us
Safe from sins which lie
Hidden by some pleasure
From our youthful eye.

5. Holy Spirit, help us
Daily by Thy Might
What is wrong to conquer
And to choose the right.

Bethany Blessing 107

Carrie Stewart-Besserer

B. D. Ackley
Arr. W. E. Yoder

Ac - cept our grat - i - tude, Lord, For all the bless - ings

Thou dost give; Di - rect and guide our dai - ly paths,

And teach us how to live. For Je - sus' sake, A - men.

Into My Heart 108

H. D. C.

Harry D. Clark
Arr. W. E. Yoder

In - to my heart, In - to my heart, Come in - to my heart, Lord Je - sus;

Come in to - day, come in to stay, Come in - to my heart, Lord Je - sus.

109 Lord, Speak to Me

FRANCES R. HAVERGAL

GEORGE HEWS
Arr. W. E. YODER

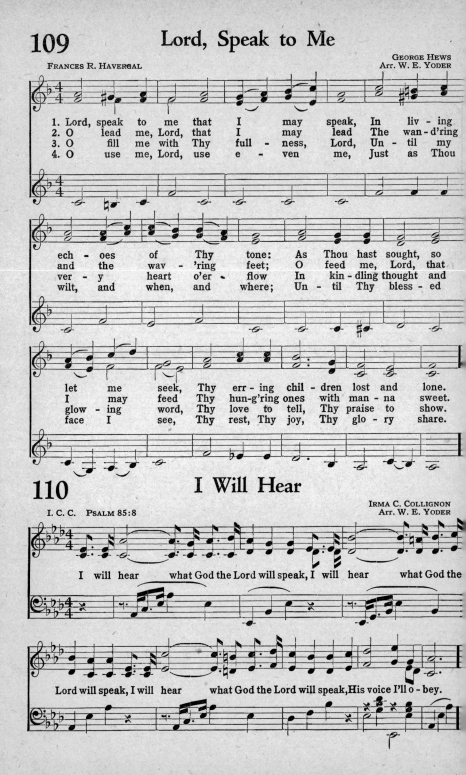

1. Lord, speak to me that I may speak, In liv-ing
2. O lead me, Lord, that I may lead The wan-d'ring
3. O fill me with Thy full - ness, Lord, Un - til my
4. O use me, Lord, use e - ven me, Just as Thou

ech - oes of Thy tone: As Thou hast sought, so
and the wav - 'ring feet; O feed me, Lord, that
ver - y heart o'er - flow In kin - dling thought and
wilt, and when, and where; Un - til Thy bless - ed

let me seek, Thy err - ing chil - dren lost and lone.
I may feed Thy hun-g'ring ones with man - na sweet.
glow - ing word, Thy love to tell, Thy praise to show.
face I see, Thy rest, Thy joy, Thy glo - ry share.

110 I Will Hear

I. C. C.   PSALM 85:8

IRMA C. COLLIGNON
Arr. W. E. YODER

I will hear what God the Lord will speak, I will hear what God the
Lord will speak, I will hear what God the Lord will speak, His voice I'll o - bey.

Fling Wide the Portals

111

GEO. WEISSEL
CATHERINE WINKWORTH, Tr.

J. BAPTISTE CALKIN
Arr. W. E. YODER

1. Fling wide the por-tals of your heart! Make it a tem-ple, set a-part
2. Re-deem-er, come! I o-pen wide My heart to Thee: here, Lord, a-bide!

From earth-ly use for heav'n's em-ploy, A-dorned with pray'r and love and joy.
Let me Thy in-ner pres-ence feel: Thy grace and love in me re-veal.

We Give Thee but Thine Own

112

W. WALSHAM HOW

ROB. SCHUMANN
Arr. W. E. YODER

1. We give Thee but Thine own, What-e'er the gift may be; All
2. May we Thy boun-ties thus As stew-ards true re-ceive, And
3. And we be-lieve Thy Word, Though dim our faith may be, When

that we have is Thine a-lone, A trust, O Lord, from Thee.
glad-ly, as Thou bless-est us, To Thee our of-f'rings give.
we with oth-ers share, O Lord, We do it un-to Thee.

113 Take My Life and Let It Be

FRANCES R. HAVERGAL

CESAR MALAN
Arr. W. E. YODER

1. Take my life and let it be Con - se - crat - ed
2. Take my feet and let them be Swift and beau - ti -
3. Take my sil - ver and my gold, Not a mite would
4. Take my lips and let them be Filled with mes - sag -
5. Take my will and make it Thine; It shall be no

Lord to Thee; Take my hands and let them move At the
ful for Thee; Take my voice, and let me sing Al - ways
I with - hold; Take my mo - ments and my days, Let them
es for Thee; Take my in - tel - lect, and use Ev - 'ry
long - er mine; Take my heart, it is Thine own! It shall

im - pulse of Thy love, At the im - pulse of Thy love.
on - ly for my King, Al - ways on - ly for my King.
flow in end - less praise, Let them flow in end - less praise.
power as Thou shalt choose, Ev - 'ry power as Thou shalt choose.
be Thy roy - al throne, It shall be Thy roy - al throne.

114 I Thank the Lord My Maker

Tune: Use No. 122

I thank the Lord my Maker
For all His gifts to me;
For making me partaker
Of bounties rich and free;
For father and for mother,
Who give me clothes and food,
For sister and for brother,
And all the kind and good.

THOMAS MACKELLAR

My Body is God's Temple

Elizabeth A. Showalter

George F. Root
Arr. W. E. Yoder

1. My bod - y is God's tem - ple; I'm build - ing ev - 'ry day,
2. My mind shall be God's work - shop; That ev - 'ry thought and word
3. My soul is God's pos - ses - sion, Kept by Him ev - 'ry hour,

In home, and church, and school - room, By stud - ies, work, and play.
And deed be kind and no - ble, And hon - or Christ, my Lord.
For - giv - en, cleansed, and quick - en'd, By His re - deem - ing pow'r.

I know if I build wise - ly, Re - fus - ing all that's wrong,
I know if I think tru - ly, Test - ing the things I do,
I know that if I trust Him, Walk close - ly by His side,

My tem - ple will grow love - ly, For God both pure and strong.
My mind will grow more like His, My deeds more like His, too.
My soul will have com - mun - ion With God, what - e'er be - tide.

116
If God Be for Us

ROMANS 8:31

WALTER G. TAYLOR
Arr. W. E. YODER

If God be for us, Who can be a-gainst us, Who can

be a-gainst us, who can be a-gainst us? If God be for us,

Who can be a-gainst us? No one, no one, no one!
no one, no one,

117
Nothing Too Hard

JEREMIAH 32:17

ARR. W. E. YODER

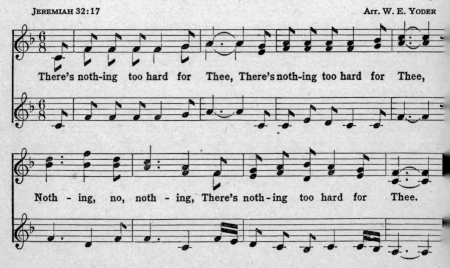

There's noth-ing too hard for Thee, There's noth-ing too hard for Thee,

Noth - ing, no, noth - ing, There's noth-ing too hard for Thee.

MARY RUTH MISHLER

1. No warm down-y pil - low His sweet head press'd, No
2. No ju - bi - lant clang of re - joic - ing bell The
3. Thou Heav'n-ly Stran-ger so gen - tle and mild, Though

soft silk - en gar - ments His fair form dress'd, He
glo - ri - ous news to the world did tell, But
born in a man - ger the Fa-ther's own child, We'll

lay in a man - ger, This heav - en - ly stran - ger;
an - gels from glo - ry Sang sweet - ly the sto - ry
wor - ship be - fore Thee And praise and a - dore Thee

The lit - tle Lord Je - sus, The won - der - ful child.
Of Beth - le - hem's strang - er The Sav - iour of men.
And sing the glad sto - ry A - gain and a - gain.

119 O Come, Little Children

CHRISTOPH VON SCHMID
GAIL B. BURKET, Tr.

J. P. A. SCHULTZ
Arr. W. E. YODER

1. O come, lit-tle chil-dren, O come and be-hold,
2. En-cir-cled with glo-ry The ho-ly Child lies,
3. And now, to the man-ger, What gift shall we bring

The man-ger is cra-dling The Babe, as of old,
While myr-iads of an-gels Re-joice in the skies.
To show our great love for The heav-en-ly King?

Blest Ma-ry and Jo-seph Bend o-ver Him there;
O join with the an-gels In ju-bi-lant lays,
He cares for no treas-ure Of earth or of mart.

And shep-herds are kneel-ing De-vout-ly in prayer.
O sing till your voic-es Re-ech-o their praise.
O give Him de-vo-tion: O give Him your heart.

Who Is He in Yonder Stall? 120

B. R. HANBY

BENJ. R. HANBY
Arr. W. E. YODER

1. Who is He in yon - der stall, At whose feet the shep - herds fall?
2. Who is He in yon - der cot Bend - ing to His toil - some lot?

REFRAIN

'Tis the Lord, oh won - drous sto - ry! 'Tis the Lord, the King of glo - ry, At His feet we hum - bly fall, Crown Him, crown Him Lord of all.

3. Who is He in deep distress Fasting in the wilderness?

4. Lo, at midnight who is He Prays in dark Gethsemane?

5. Who is He in Calvary's throes, Asks for blessings on His foes?

6. Who is He that from the grave Comes to heal and help and save?

7. Who is He that from yon throne Rules the world of light alone?

121 O Jesus, Once a Nazareth Boy

Stanza 1, Anon.
Stanza 2, ETHEL W. TROUT

HENRY S. CUTLER
Arr. W. E. YODER

1. O Je - sus, once a Naza - reth boy, And tempt - ed like as we,
2. O Je - sus, once a Naza - reth boy, Who toiled through hap-py days,

All in - ward foes help us de-stroy, And spot-less all to be.
May we our dai - ly tasks en - joy, And work, with songs of praise.

We trust Thee for the grace to win Our way through trial and wrong:
At school, at home we fol - low Thee, And glad - ly do our part;

Lord Je - sus help us con - quer sin And serve Thee all day long.
Work hard, play fair, and try to be Hap - py and pure in heart.

My Master Was a Worker 122

WILLIAM GEORGE TARRANT, 1853
Adapted by ELIZABETH A. SHOWALTER

GEORGE J. WEBB, 1837
Arr. W. E. YODER

1. My Mas-ter was a work-er, with dai-ly work to do,
2. My Mas-ter was a com-rade, a trust-y friend and true,
3. My Mas-ter was a help-er, the woes of life He knew,
4. Then broth-er, brave and man-ly, to-geth-er let us be,

And he who would be like Him, must be a work-er, too;
And he who would be like Him, must be a com-rade, too;
And he who would be like Him, must be a help-er, too;
For He, who is our Mas-ter, the Man of men was He;

Then wel-come hon-est la-bor, and hon-est la-bor's fare,
In hap-py hours of sing-ing, in si-lent hours of care,
The bur-den will grow light-er, if each for each will bear,
The men who would be like Him are want-ed ev-er-y-where,

I want to be a work-er, the Mas-ter's work to share.
I want to be a com-rade, the Mas-ter's work to share.
I want to be a help-er, the Mas-ter's work to share.
But we must love each oth-er, the Mas-ter's work to share.

I Want to Be Like Jesus 123

1. I want to be like Jesus,
   As He was when a Child,
   To speak words sweet and loving,
   With temper meek and mild;
   And in the home, as He did,
   My parents to obey,
   And help by doing gladly
   My share of tasks each day.

2. I want to be like Jesus
   As He was when a Lad,
   To play as fair and kindly,
   I'll make my playmates glad;
   To be as generous always,
   My good things I will share,
   And help make people happier
   Around me everywhere.

MARY BRAINERD SMITH

By permission of Sunday School Times Co.

124 Wonderful Things to Know

H. H. L.

H. H. Lemmel

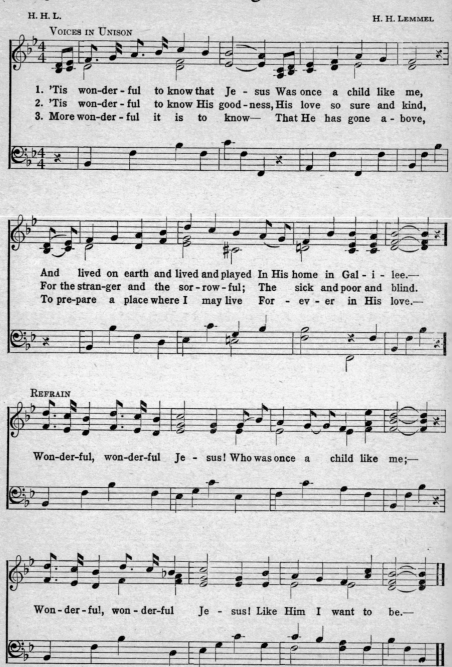

VOICES IN UNISON

1. 'Tis won-der-ful to know that Je-sus Was once a child like me,
2. 'Tis won-der-ful to know His good-ness, His love so sure and kind,
3. More won-der-ful it is to know— That He has gone a-bove,

And lived on earth and lived and played In His home in Gal-i-lee.—
For the stran-ger and the sor-row-ful; The sick and poor and blind.
To pre-pare a place where I may live For-ev-er in His love.—

REFRAIN

Won-der-ful, won-der-ful Je-sus! Who was once a child like me;—

Won-der-ful, won-der-ful Je-sus! Like Him I want to be.—

We Would See Jesus

J. EDGAR PARK

HERBERT TURNER
Arr. W. E. YODER

1. We would see Je - sus, lo! His star is shin - ing
2. We would see Je - sus, Ma - ry's Son most ho - ly,
3. We would see Je - sus, on the moun - tain teach - ing,
4. We would see Je - sus, in His work of heal - ing,
5. We would see Je - sus, in the ear - ly morn - ing,

A - bove the sta - ble while the an - gels sing;
Light of the vil - lage life from day to day;
With all the lis - tening peo - ple gath - ered round;
At e - ven - tide be - fore the sun is set:
Still as of old He call - eth, "Fol - low Me";

There in a man - ger, on the hay re - clin - ing,
Shin - ing re - vealed through ev - ery task most low - ly,
While birds and flowers and sky a - bove are preach - ing
Di - vine and hu - man, in His deep re - veal - ing
Let us a - rise, all mean - er serv - ice scorn - ing,

Haste let us lay our gifts be - fore the King.
The Christ of God, the Life, the Truth, the Way.
The bless - ed - ness which sim - ple trust has found.
Of God and man in lov - ing serv - ice met.
Lord, we are Thine, we give our - selves to Thee.

126 Miracle Song

ELSIE DUNCAN YALE

W. A. POST
Arr. W. E. YODER

1. Un - to the Lord in their blind-ness Sad, yet be - liev - ing they came,
2. Lep - ers in mis - er - y sought Him Hope-less for years had they been,
3. Jai - rus the rul - er was griev - ing Filled with anx - i - e - ty wild,
4. All of the sick of the cit - y, Help-less and crip-pled and lame,

Ask - ing His mer - cy and kind - ness, Trust-ing a - lone in His Name.
All of their bur - dens they brought Him, Cry - ing in sad-ness "Un - clean!"
Yet he came hop - ing, be - liev - ing Je - sus could heal his dear child.
Un - to the Sav-iour for pit - y, When it was e - ven-tide, came.

REFRAIN *A trifle faster*

Read - y to help! Read - y to help! The Sav - iour heard their call,

Read - y to help! Read - y to help! In love He help'd them all.

The Name of Jesus 127

W. C. MARTIN

E. S. LORENZ
Arr. W. E. YODER

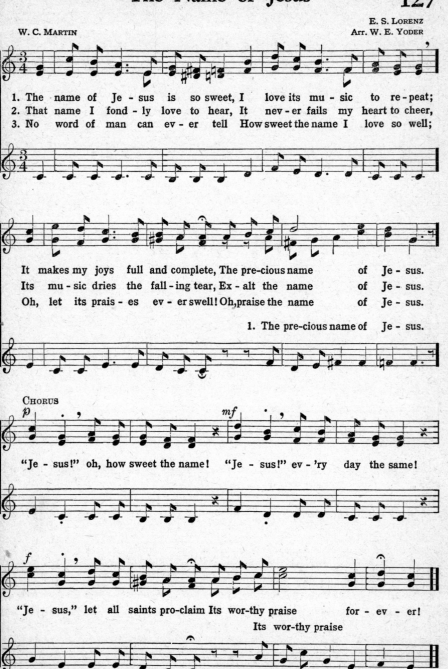

1. The name of Je - sus is so sweet, I love its mu - sic to re - peat;
2. That name I fond - ly love to hear, It nev - er fails my heart to cheer,
3. No word of man can ev - er tell How sweet the name I love so well;

It makes my joys full and complete, The pre-cious name of Je - sus.
Its mu - sic dries the fall - ing tear, Ex - alt the name of Je - sus.
Oh, let its prais - es ev - er swell! Oh, praise the name of Je - sus.

1. The pre-cious name of Je - sus.

CHORUS

p   mf

"Je - sus!" oh, how sweet the name! "Je - sus!" ev - 'ry day the same!

f

"Je - sus," let all saints pro-claim Its wor-thy praise for - ev - er!

Its wor-thy praise

128 Ye Must Be Born Again

W. T. Sleeper

Geo. C. Stebbins
Arr. W. E. Yoder

1. A rul-er once came to Je-sus by night, To ask Him the way of sal-va-tion and light; The Mas-ter made an-swer in words true and plain, "Ye must be born a-gain."

2. Ye chil-dren of men, at-tend to the word So sol-emn-ly ut-tered by Je-sus the Lord, And let not this mes-sage to you be in vain, "Ye must be born a-gain."

3. O ye who would en-ter that glo-rious rest, And sing with the ran-som'd the song of the blest, The life ev-er-last-ing if you would ob-tain, "Ye must be born a-gain."

REFRAIN

"Ye must be born a-gain, Ye must be born a-gain, I ver-i-ly, ver-i-ly, say un-to thee, Ye must be born a-gain."

Follow Me, the Master Said

129

ARTHUR COTTMAN
Arr. by W. E. YODER

Anonymous

1. "Fol - low Me" the Mas - ter said; We will fol - low Je - sus:
2. Should the world and sin op - pose, We will fol - low Je - sus:
3. Though the way may dark ap - pear, We will fol - low Je - sus:
4. Ev - er keep the end in view; We will fol - low Je - sus:

By His word and spir - it led, We will fol - low Je - sus.
He is great - er than our foes; We will fol - low Je - sus.
He will make our path - way clear; We will fol - low Je - sus.
All His prom - is - es are true; We will fol - low Je - sus.

Still for us He lives to plead, At the throne doth in - ter - cede,
On His prom - ise we de - pend; He will suc - cor and de - fend,
In our dai - ly round of care, As we plead with God in prayer,
When this earth - ly course is run, And the Mas - ter says, "Well done!"

Of - fers help in time of need: We will fol - low Je - sus.
Help and keep us to the end; We will fol - low Je - sus.
With the cross which we must bear, We will fol - low Je - sus.
Life e - ter - nal we have won: We will fol - low Je - sus.

130 Beautiful Saviour

Tune: Fairest Lord Jesus

German 17th Century

Arr. by WALTER E. YODER

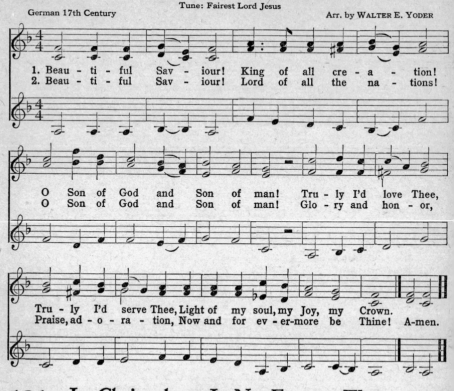

1. Beau - ti - ful Sav - iour! King of all cre - a - tion!
2. Beau - ti - ful Sav - iour! Lord of all the na - tions!

O Son of God and Son of man! Tru - ly I'd love Thee,
O Son of God and Son of man! Glo - ry and hon - or,

Tru - ly I'd serve Thee, Light of my soul, my Joy, my Crown.
Praise, ad - o - ra - tion, Now and for ev - er-more be Thine! A - men.

131 In Christ there Is No East or West

JOHN OXENHAM

ALEX. R. REINAGLE
Arr. W. E. YODER

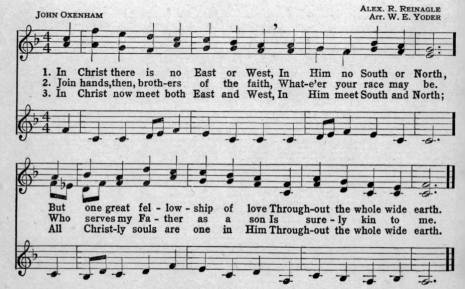

1. In Christ there is no East or West, In Him no South or North,
2. Join hands, then, broth-ers of the faith, What-e'er your race may be.
3. In Christ now meet both East and West, In Him meet South and North;

But one great fel - low - ship of love Through-out the whole wide earth.
Who serves my Fa - ther as a son Is sure - ly kin to me.
All Christ-ly souls are one in Him Through-out the whole wide earth.

O Word of God Incarnate

132

W. WALSHAM HOWE

FELIX MENDELSSOHN
Arr. W. E. YODER

1. O Word of God in-car-nate, O Wis-dom from on high,
2. The Church from her dear Mas-ter Re-ceived the gift di-vine,
3. It float-eth like a ban-ner Be-fore God's host un-furled;
4. O make Thy Church, dear Sav-iour, A lamb of pur-est gold,

O Truth, un-changed, un-chang-ing, O Light of our dark sky;
And still that light she lift-eth O'er all the earth to shine.
It shin-eth like a bea-con A-bove the dark-ling world;
To bear be-fore the na-tions Thy true light as of old;

We praise Thee for the ra-diance That from the hal-lowed page,
It is the gold-en cas-ket Where gems of truth are stored,
It is the chart and com-pass That o'er life's surg-ing sea,
O teach Thy wan-d'ring pil-grims By this their path to trace,

A lan-tern to our foot-steps Shines on from age to age.
It is the heav'n-drawn pic-ture Of Christ, the liv-ing Word.
'Mid mists and rocks and quick-sands, Still guide, O Christ, to Thee.
Till, clouds and dark-ness end-ed, They see Thee face to face.

133 The Word of God Shall Guide My Feet

Nancy Byrd Turner, 1926   Grace Wilbur Conant, 1926

The Word of God shall guide my feet, Wher - ev - er I may go;

The Word of God shall teach my heart The things it ought to know;

The Word of God shall make me strong And bless me through my

whole life long, And bless me through my whole life long. A - men.

Book Divine

JOHN BURTON, JR.

XAVIER S. VON WARTENSEE
Arr. W. E. YODER

134

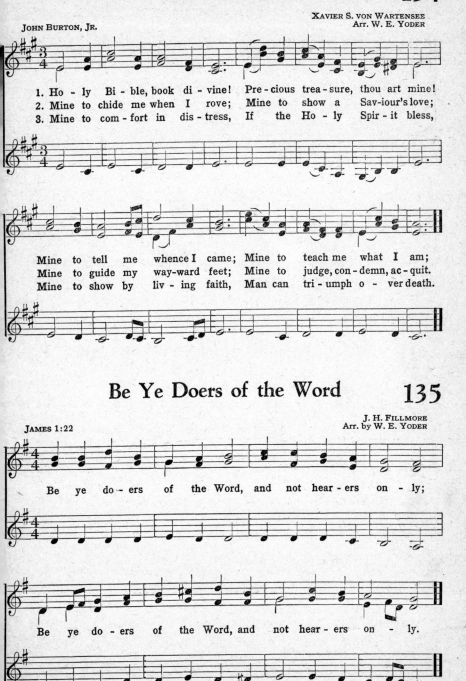

1. Ho - ly Bi - ble, book di - vine! Pre - cious trea - sure, thou art mine!
2. Mine to chide me when I rove; Mine to show a Sav-iour's love;
3. Mine to com - fort in dis - tress, If the Ho - ly Spir - it bless,

Mine to tell me whence I came; Mine to teach me what I am;
Mine to guide my way-ward feet; Mine to judge, con - demn, ac - quit.
Mine to show by liv - ing faith, Man can tri - umph o - ver death.

Be Ye Doers of the Word

J. H. FILLMORE
Arr. by W. E. YODER

135

JAMES 1:22

Be ye do - ers of the Word, and not hear - ers on - ly;

Be ye do - ers of the Word, and not hear - ers on - ly.

136 God's Word in Your Heart

ROBERT HARKNESS
Arr. W. E. YODER

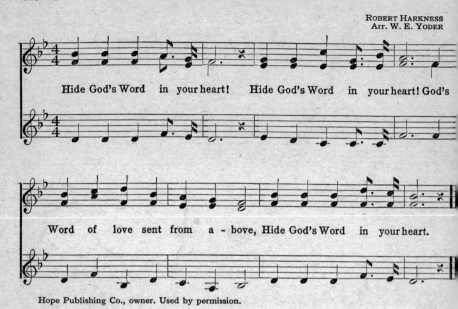

Hide God's Word in your heart! Hide God's Word in your heart! God's

Word of love sent from a-bove, Hide God's Word in your heart.

Hope Publishing Co., owner. Used by permission.

137 Bread of Heaven, On Thee We Feed

JOSIAH CONDER

WM. BRADBURY
Arr. W. E. YODER

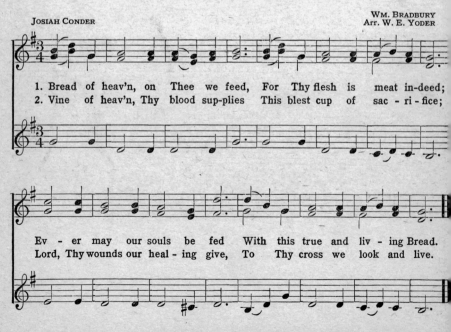

1. Bread of heav'n, on Thee we feed, For Thy flesh is meat in-deed;
2. Vine of heav'n, Thy blood sup-plies This blest cup of sac-ri-fice;

Ev-er may our souls be fed With this true and liv-ing Bread.
Lord, Thy wounds our heal-ing give, To Thy cross we look and live.

THE CRUCIFIXION

Come, We that Love the Lord 138

Isaac Watts

G. F. Handel
Arr. W. E. Yoder

1. Come, we that love the Lord, And let our joys be known;
2. Let those re-fuse to sing, Who nev-er knew our God;

Join in a song with sweet ac-cord, And thus sur-round the throne.
But chil-dren of the heav'n-ly King, May speak their joys a-broad.

How Lovely are the Messengers 139

(From St. Paul)

Felix Mendelssohn
Arr. by W. E. Yoder

Andante con moto

How love-ly are the mes-sen-gers That teach us the gos-pel of peace, How love-ly

are the mes-sen-gers That preach us the gos-pel of peace, The gos-pel of peace.

140 One Holy Church of God

SAMUEL LONGFELLOW

W. CROFT
Arr. W. E. YODER

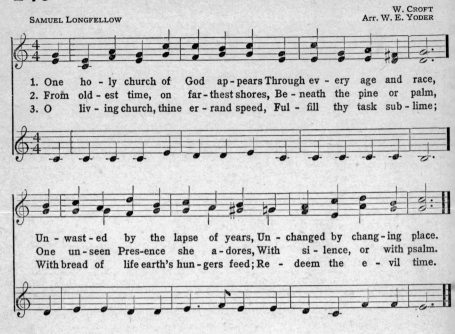

1. One ho - ly church of God ap - pears Through ev - ery age and race,
2. From old - est time, on far - thest shores, Be - neath the pine or palm,
3. O liv - ing church, thine er - rand speed, Ful - fill thy task sub - lime;

Un - wast - ed by the lapse of years, Un - changed by chang - ing place.
One un - seen Pres-ence she a - dores, With si - lence, or with psalm.
With bread of life earth's hun - gers feed; Re - deem the e - vil time.

141 The Church of God Is Calling

ELIZABETH McE. SHIELDS

ELDA FLETT BAKER
Arr. W. E. YODER

1. The church of God is call - ing, Is call - ing each to bring
2. We hear the call to du - ty, And glad - ly will we bring

A loy - al heart and serv - ice, To Christ, our Lord and King.
Our loy - al hearts and serv - ice, To Christ, our Lord and King.

The Son of God Goes Forth to War 142

REGINALD HEBER

HENRY S. CUTLER
Arr. W. E. YODER

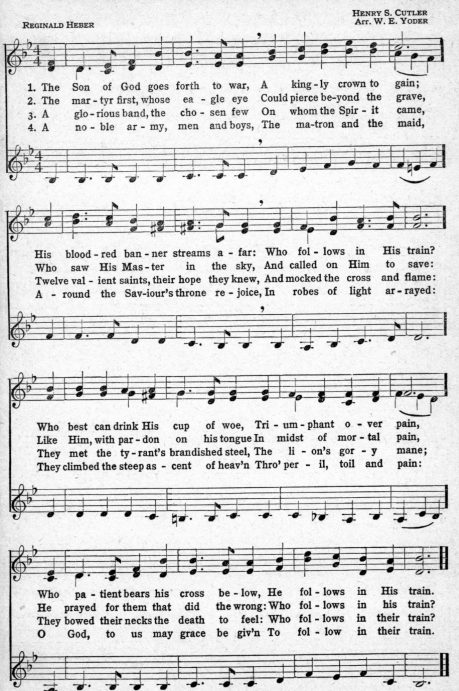

1. The Son of God goes forth to war, A king-ly crown to gain;
2. The mar-tyr first, whose ea-gle eye Could pierce be-yond the grave,
3. A glo-rious band, the cho-sen few On whom the Spir-it came,
4. A no-ble ar-my, men and boys, The ma-tron and the maid,

His blood-red ban-ner streams a-far: Who fol-lows in His train?
Who saw His Mas-ter in the sky, And called on Him to save:
Twelve val-iant saints, their hope they knew, And mocked the cross and flame:
A-round the Sav-iour's throne re-joice, In robes of light ar-rayed:

Who best can drink His cup of woe, Tri-um-phant o-ver pain,
Like Him, with par-don on his tongue In midst of mor-tal pain,
They met the ty-rant's brandished steel, The li-on's gor-y mane;
They climbed the steep as-cent of heav'n Thro' per-il, toil and pain:

Who pa-tient bears his cross be-low, He fol-lows in His train.
He prayed for them that did the wrong: Who fol-lows in his train?
They bowed their necks the death to feel: Who fol-lows in their train?
O God, to us may grace be giv'n To fol-low in their train.

143 Living for Jesus

THOMAS O. CHISHOLM

C. HAROLD LOWDEN
Arr. W. E. YODER

1. Liv - ing for Je - sus a life that is true,
2. Liv - ing for Je - sus who died in my place,
3. Liv - ing for Je - sus wher - ev - er I am,

Striv - ing to please Him in all that I do:
Bear - ing on Cal - v'ry my sin and dis - grace,
Do - ing each du - ty in His ho - ly name;

Yield - ing al - le - giance glad heart - ed and free,
Such love con - strains me to an - swer His call,
Will - ing to suf - fer af - flic - tion and loss,

This is the path - way of bless - ing for me.
Fol - low His lead - ing and give Him my all.
Deem - ing each tri - al a part of my cross.

Anywhere With Jesus

144

J. H. Brown and Mrs. C. M. Alexander

D. B. Towner
Arr. W. E. Yoder

1. An-y-where with Je-sus I can safe-ly go, An-y-where He
2. An-y-where with Je-sus I am not a-lone, Oth-er friends may
3. An-y-where with Je-sus I can go to sleep When the dark'ning

leads me in this world be-low; An-y-where with-out Him dear-est
fail me, He is still my own; Tho' His hand may lead me o-ver
shad-ows round a-bout me creep, Know-ing I shall wak-en nev-er

joys would fade, An-y-where with Je-sus I am not a-fraid.
drear-est ways, An-y-where with Je-sus is a house of praise.
more to roam, An-y-where with Je-sus will be home sweet home.

Chorus

An-y-where! An-y-where! Fear I can-not know;

An-y-where with Je-sus I can safe-ly go.

145 True-Hearted, Whole-Hearted

FRANCES R. HAVERGAL

GEO. C. STEBBINS
Arr. W. E. YODER

1. True-heart-ed, whole-heart-ed, faith-ful and loy-al, King of our lives, by Thy
2. True-heart-ed, whole-heart-ed, full-est al-le-giance, Yielding hence-forth to our
3. True-heart-ed, whole-heart-ed, Sav-ior all glo-rious! Take Thy great pow-er and

grace we will be; Un-der the stan-dard ex-alt-ed and roy-al,
glo-ri-ous King; Val-iant en-deav-or and lov-ing o-be-dience,
reign there a-lone, O-ver our wills and af-fec-tions vic-to-rious,

CHORUS

Strong in Thy strength we will bat-tle for Thee. Peal out the watch-word!
Free-ly and joy-ous-ly now would we bring. Peal
Free-ly sur-ren-dered and whol-ly Thine own. Peal

si-lence it nev-er! Song of our spir-its, re-joic-ing and free; Peal out the
si-lence Song re-joic-ing Peal

watch-word loy-al for-ev-er, King of our lives, By Thy grace we will be.
loy-al King

The King's Business

146

Dr. E. T. Cassel

Flora H. Cassel
Arr. W. E. Yoder

1. I am a stran-ger here with-in a for-eign land, My home is far a-way, up-on a gold-en strand; Am-bas-sa-dor to be of realms be-yond the sea, I'm here on busi-ness for my King.

2. This is the King's com-mand, that all men ev-'ry-where, Re-pent and turn a-way, from sin's se-duc-tive snare; That all who will o-bey, with Him shall reign for aye, And that's my business for my King.

3. My home is bright-er far than Shar-on's ros-y plain, E-ter-nal life and joy through-out its vast do-main; My Sov'reign bids me tell how mor-tals there may dwell, And that's my business for my King.

REFRAIN

This is the mes-sage that I bring, A mes-sage an-gels fain would sing; "Oh, be ye re-con-ciled," Thus saith my Lord and King, "Oh, be ye re-con-ciled to God."

147 From Greenland's Icy Mountains

REGINALD HEBER

LOWELL MASON
Arr. W. E. YODER

1. From Green-land's i - cy moun - tains, From In - dia's cor - al strand,
2. What though the spi - cy breez - es Blow soft o'er Cey - lon's isle;
3. Can we, whose souls are light - ed With wis - dom from on high,
4. Waft, waft, ye winds, His sto - ry, And you, ye wa - ters, roll,

Where Af - ric's sun - ny foun - tains Roll down their gold - en sand,
Though ev - 'ry pros - pect pleas - es, And on - ly man is vile?
Can we to men be - night - ed The lamp of life de - ny?
Till like a sea of glo - ry It spreads from pole to pole;

From many an an - cient riv - er, From many a palm - y plain,
In vain with lav - ish kind - ness The gifts of God are strown;
Sal - va - tion! O sal - va - tion! The joy - ful sound pro - claim,
Till o'er our ran - somed na - ture The Lamb for sin - ners slain,

They call us to de - liv - er Their land from er - ror's chain.
The hea - then in His blind - ness Bows down to wood and stone.
Till each re - mot - est na - tion Has learnt Mes - si - ah's name.
Re - deem - er, King, Cre - a - tor, In bliss re - turns to reign.